Race Walk Clinic - in a Book

by

Jeff Salvage

Tim Seaman

Second Edition

Copyright 2011, Walking Promotions

Medford, NJ

ISBN: 9781466282759

Table of Contents

Chapter One - Introduction 3

Chapter Two - Effort 5

Chapter Three - Textbook Technique 11

Chapter Four - Legality Issues 23

    Correcting Loss of Contact (Lifting) 31

    Correcting Bent-Knee Issues 42

    Being Overly Legal 60

Chapter Five - Hip Issues 67

    Correcting Minimal Forward Hip Rotation 67

    Correcting Excessive Hip Drop 75

Chapter Six - Leg Issues 83

    Correcting High Knee Drive 83

    Correcting Overstriding 86

    Correcting a Wide Stance 87

    Correcting Foot and Knee Crossover 88

    Correcting Improper Swing Foot Carriage 90

Chapter Seven - Arm, Hand, and Shoulder Issues 91

    Correcting Arm Carriage Issues 94

    Correcting Hand Issues 97

    Correcting Shoulder Issues 98

Chapter Eight - Posture Issues 103

    Correcting Leaning Forward 103

    Correcting Leaning Backward 110

Epilogue 115

Chapter One
Introduction

Elite race walkers move with a fluidity and grace that are the envy of anyone who has tried the low-impact, yet high-intensity sport of race walking. Capable of traveling in excess of 10 miles per hour, they zip along with rhythmic synchronicity as their arms, legs, and hips drive them forward efficiently, utilizing 95 percent of their muscles. Do you want to walk with similar grace? With a dearth of knowledgeable coaches and clinicians across the U.S., many race walkers looking to improve their technique turn to the Internet, books, or DVDs for guidance. While these resources are helpful, they mainly focus on what to do right and what you may be doing wrong. What is missing is *remediation*; they do not focus on *how* to correct your improper technique. It's easy to say "use your hips more," but most race walkers do not understand how to accomplish this.

The concept for *Race Walk Clinic — in a Book* grew from the comments received after a very successful Seaman and Salvage race walking clinic. Our clinics combine the vast knowledge of one of America's premier race walkers, two-time Olympian Tim Seaman, with the award-winning instructional and promotional experience of Jeff Salvage. Salvage is *racewalk.com's* founder and the author of the *Race Walk Like a Champion* book and DVD. While the clinic attendees loved the material taught, they wanted a written summary to help them retain what they learned. *Race Walk Clinic — in a Book* is the answer to those requests. For all those who can't come to one of our clinics and for all those who do come but want to walk away with their newly gained knowledge in print, *Race Walk Clinic — in a Book* is for you.

Our approach in *Race Walk Clinic — in a Book* is to pick up where other training materials leave off. We start by grounding our discussion with a review of correct race walking technique, but do not focus on the many aspects of technique that you can do incorrectly. Next we divide race walking technique problems into broad categories, starting with issues of legality and then separating technique issues into categories such as hip, leg, arm, and posture problems. For each category we illustrate the problem with photographs of either elite race walkers or (for beginner problems) staged images. We then offer remediation in two forms: exercises, drills, and stretches to improve your style, and mental cues to guide your focus while race walking.

Within the educational material presented, we've interspersed "Tales from the Track," a unique collection of stories in which great race walkers from the U.S. and around the world retell some of their most memorable experiences.

Acknowledgments

Race Walk Clinic — in a Book does not contain just the combined knowledge of Tim Seaman and Jeff Salvage, but the combined knowledge of ourselves as well as those who influenced and built our foundation of race walking knowledge. Some of our biggest influences were Ken Hendler, Gary Westerfield, Troy Engle, Frank Alongi, Jake Jacobson, Tom Eastler, Mario Fiore, Jim DiSalvo, Frank Manhardt, Bohdan Bulakowski, Enrique Peña, Mike DeWitt, Stephan Platzer, Allen James, Kevin Eastler, A.C. Jaime, Paul Mascali, Ray Kuhles, Curt Clausen, Andrew Hermann, and of course Jefferson Perez.

Special thanks go to the Flagstaff Athletic Club for allowing us the use of their facilities during the photographing of this book, Chris Robinson, MPT, for his insights on the many exercises listed in this book, and finally to Bruce Barron for his help editing this text and Eugene Geer for his photograph of Jeff Salvage.

Dedication

This book is dedicated to the two men without whom neither of us would have ever race walked: Coach Ken Hendler and Coach Frank Manhardt.

Chapter Two
Effort

Race walking competitively is not your Sunday stroll in the park. It requires a great deal of effort to compete successfully. The effort comes in many forms, including a unique combination of extreme physical exertion and mental focus.

People often ask if it is hard to race walk. If time is a measure, race walking wins hands down. It is the longest footrace at the Olympics; a 50km race walk can be completed in 3:34 vs. running a marathon which takes 2:03. Therefore, race walkers must exert effort significantly longer than their running counterparts. If instead you use heart rate as a measure, race walking is pretty hard. An elite male race walker completes a 20km in under 1:20 and averages a heart rate between 180 and 190 beats per minute (bpm). For a 50km, the best in the world finish it in less than 3:40 and have an average heart rate between 160 and 170 bpm. That may seem high, but that's nothing compared to what can be achieved while working out. A young, elite race walker can clock as high as 220 bpm. Race walking gets the heart working just as well as running does, but without excessive jarring to the body. Race walking is also more difficult if you measure difficulty by calories burned. Since race walking is less efficient than running, it means race walkers burn more calories per mile than runners. Over the course of a 50km, that's a lot of calories. Finally, if you measure difficulty by concentration, both runners and walkers push their bodies to the limit, but runners do not have to worry about being disqualified for poor form. Race walkers, on the other hand, are constantly watched, especially when they are pushing the hardest.

Given these considerations, the total exertion of race walking is arguably greater than that of running. This exertion calls for effort — a simple word with multiple meanings. To become stronger, effort is applied in the form of training; to walk faster, effort is applied in the form of exertion; to improve technique, effort is applied in the form of practice, remedial drills, concentration and, well, more practice.

When we were beginning race walkers, we mistakenly thought that as we got in better shape, racing would get easier. We couldn't have been more wrong. As we trained more, our engine got bigger and the effort that we were capable of grew immensely. Remember when you just started to learn to race walk. Do you remember your legs getting really sore, but your lungs were not tired? We also remember thinking that if we just got stronger, we could cruise effortlessly along to faster times. Then one day it was as if someone flipped a switch, our legs felt better and our lungs were gasping for air. Apparently, we are not alone. Over the next few pages, observe photographs taken at the Olympic Trials, World Cup, and Olympic Games. These athletes embody effort. While there are exceptions like four-time gold medalist Robert Korzeniowski, most athletes' exertion clearly shows by the end of the race. When you are tired and ready to succumb to the demon of fatigue, robbing you of your personal best, remember these photographs. Remember their effort and apply the same. As Gary Westerfield once said, "Nothing hurts more than a bad race." He was correct. The pain of exertion goes away shortly after you stop; the pain of disappointment due to a lack of effort can last a lifetime.

Francisco Fernandez of Spain demonstrating that the effort was worth it after winning the 20km race at the 2006 World Cup in La Coruña, Spain

Ecuador's Jefferson Perez, 1996 Olympic champion, shown pushing hard at the 20km World Cup in 2006

Eddy Riva of France giving it all as he finishes 28th in the 50km at the 2008 Beijing Olympics

Joanne Dow, exhausted after finishing 2nd in the 2004 U.S. Olympic Trials

Olga Kaniskina of Russia at the 2006 World Cup. Two years later she crushed the field at the 2008 Beijing Olympics.

María Vasco of Spain finishing 5th in the 2008 Beijing Olympics 20km race walk

Athanasia Tsoumeleka (2027) pulls away from Jane Saville and Olimpiada Ivanova to win the women's 20K race walk at the 2004 Athens Olympics

We start this book discussing effort because no improvement as a race walker can come without effort. Many people learn how to do dynamic drills but rarely incorporate them as an integral part of their training regimen. Many know they need to raise or lower their arms, but rarely do they focus on their arm swing throughout their workout. Many know they need to stretch properly after a workout, but often they allow life to interfere with what is best.

Reading this book alone will not improve your technique. You must practice continually what we recommend so that your muscles are trained to move in the proper manner. "If it was easy, everyone would make the Olympics," former U.S. National Team member Paul Schwartzberg used to say. It's not easy to get faster and more efficient. It requires hard work and perseverance. That said, if you put forth the effort to practice what we teach in *Race Walk Clinic — in a Book*, you'll improve your race times, look more graceful doing it, and reduce your risk of injury.

TALES FROM THE TRACK

While shooting the photographs for this text, we bumped into the coaching legend Jack Daniels. Author of the book *Daniels' Running Formula*, Daniels is considered one of the world's leading experts on exercise physiology. What did this esteemed authority of physiology volunteer about race walking? He shared with us a fact that neither of us knew: according to his tests, race walkers have a higher anaerobic threshold (i.e., ability to use available oxygen efficiently) than runners. Score one for us!

Chapter Three
Textbook Technique

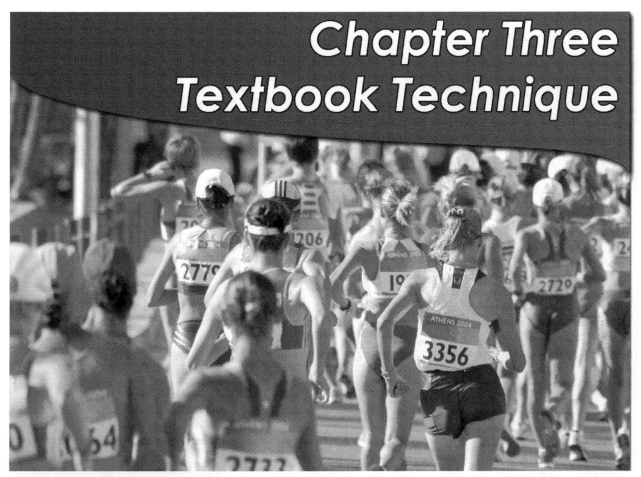

Figure 3-1. Robert Korzeniowski (#2679) on his way to a gold medal in the 50km race walk at the 2004 Athens Olympic Games

The definition of race walking is fairly concise. Here is the two-part definition used by the international track and field community and by USA Track and Field to govern race walking:

• Race walking is a progression of steps so taken that the walker makes contact with the ground so that no visible (to the human eye) loss of contact occurs.

• The advancing leg must be straightened (i.e., not bent at the knee) from the moment of first contact with the ground until in the vertical upright position.

However, understand the nuances and complexities of efficient race walking technique is far from simple. Watching four-time Olympic gold medalist Robert Korzeniowski blaze by leaves you awestruck. It also leaves you with an image of textbook form that is fluid, powerful, and graceful. While many positive adjectives can replace those stated, they don't describe why he looks so good. The key to Korzeniowski's form is a combination of strength, flexibility, and range of motion. While most of us think about the first two of these, it's the last one that really defines great race walking technique. It's also one reason why, even though it can be argued that Korzeniowski is reasonably off the ground at full speed, he rarely gets disqualification calls.

Perfect form for Korzeniowski wasn't always the case. While in contention for a medal at the 1992 Olympic Games, Korzeniowski was disqualified as he was about to enter the stadium. The disappointment of losing a medal focused Korzeniowski to work on his technique every day so that he would not repeat his mistake. You need to do the same.

We know we should relax when we walk, yet many of us tighten up, especially in the shoulders, when we walk hard. What happens when we tighten up? We reduce our range of motion, making it impossible to maximize efficiency. Whether it's high shoulders, holding the arms at a tight angle, or minimal hip rotation, all of these behaviors limit our range of motion, depriving our bodies of the power we need to race walk at our peak performance.

This chapter focuses on defining proper textbook form. In doing so, it highlights elite walkers demonstrating proper and improper technique. Yes, even the elites have issues they need to work on. Note that we do not focus on how to correct these problems in this chapter. Instead, the following chapters highlight drills and exercises to remediate poor technique.

POSTURE

Figure 3-2. Jared Tallent demonstrating proper posture and stride ratio in route to one of his two medals at the Beijing Olympics.

A race walker's posture is quite simple, although it wasn't always so. An elite race walker maintains an upright posture throughout the stride. The torso should not swing forward or back, nor should it twist as the hips rotate forward.

Previous to Salvage and Westerfield's 1996 publication of *Walk Like an Athlete,* American books and coaches preached leaning forward. In some cases this lean was estimated to be five percent. Leaning forward restricts hip rotation and places an incredible strain on the lower back.

Observe Figure 3-2 showing Jared Tallent walking to a silver medal in the 2008 Olympics 50km race. Tallent's posture is straight up and down, leading to more graceful and efficient technique as well as the proper stride ratio. Race walkers should have more of their stride behind them than in front of their body. Estimates vary between a 60-40 split and a 70-30 split. Tallent's sweet spot is directly in between at 64/36. Of course, there is a certain amount of subjectivity based upon where you draw the line.

LEGS

Observe Figures 3-3 to 3-8. They illustrate the correct positioning of the legs from the instant Tim Seaman's left leg strikes the ground, as his body passes directly over the leg and beyond, until his left foot is about to leave the ground behind his body.

Figure 3-3 *Figure 3-4* *Figure 3-5*

Figure 3-6 *Figure 3-7* *Figure 3-8*

Look at Figure 3-3, where his heel has just made contact with the ground. A few things happened simultaneously. Just before contact, as his leg was swinging forward, it straightened, with toes pointed up (between 30 to 45 degrees from the ground). Nearly simultaneously with those actions, his heel struck the ground. Achieving this smooth, synchronized action is the key to success.

Between Figure 3-3 and Figure 3-8, the body moves forward, over the left leg. This is where walkers tend to violate the definition of race walking. The leg must remain straightened until it is in the vertical position as shown in Figure 3-5.

Once the leg is beyond the vertical position, as in Figure 3-6, it may bend. However, when it comes time to lift your foot off the ground, if your leg is still straightened, you get an extra thrust forward by pushing off your rear foot (Figure 3-7). With proper flexibility and strength your leg stays straightened longer and you obtain this advantageous thrust. Ideally, the leg remains straightened until the heel of your rear foot lifts off the ground.

Figure 3-8 is just after your effective push off and just before rear-foot toe off, with an obvious bend in the leg. It is impossible to race walk with any efficiency and keep the leg straight as it swings forward. Notice that as his rear (left) leg leaves the ground, Tim's front (right) leg is already in position. Also, note (as we observed with Jared Tallent) that the legs do not create a symmetrical triangle. More of Tim's stride is behind his body than in front. This is achieved through proper hip action, which is explained shortly.

Figures 3-9 through 3-14 show the foot swinging through as low to the ground as possible. This averts loss of contact problems that might occur if you drive your foot too high coming through your stride. If your foot is too high, you might have a propensity to drive the leg up instead of forward, thus making you at risk of visible loss of contact and getting disqualified. Figures 3-9 through 3-14 show Tim's progression as his rear foot leaves the ground (Figure 3-10) until just after the same foot strikes the ground in front of the body (Figure 3-14). When his rear foot leaves the ground, it swings forward with the leg flexed at the knee (Figures 3-10 to 3-12). Note the constant angle between his upper and lower leg during this phase. Once he begins straightening his leg as it moves forward, he uses his quadriceps to extend it (Figures 3-13 and 3-14). Once his foot makes contact with the ground, his leg must be straightened and no longer flexed at the knee (Figure 3-14).

TALES FROM THE TRACK

Do you get harassed when you are training to race walk? It seems the abuse is a universal presence worldwide. Chris Ericson (1079 in the photo) of Australia reports that the abuse from Down Under comes from a more educated crowd of cat callers. Often Ericson hears bystanders yelling, "You're gonna get a red card." Perhaps this enlightenment is due to Australia's recent wealth of race walking success, as this country has reaped four medals in the last two Olympics. Ericson admits he doesn't just take it; he'll dish it back, having a canned response ready for almost every crack. One of his favorites is that when construction workers razz him, he replies, "Keep working boys, your taxes are paying our salary." He has others, but kids will read this book, so we'll keep it clean.

—*Chris Ericson, 2008 Olympian, Beijing, China*

Figure 3-9 *Figure 3-10* *Figure 3-11*

Figure 3-12 *Figure 3-13* *Figure 3-14*

CARRY THAT KNEE LOW

To remain efficient, race walkers must pay careful attention to how their legs swing forward after push off. Your leg should move forward with the knee as low to the ground as possible. While some upward motion is necessary to lift the foot off the ground, it should be minimized. Therefore, when the rear foot lifts up, it rises only an inch or two off the ground. This is seen throughout Figures 3-9 to 3-14. By the time your foot swings under your body, it is almost parallel with the ground (Figure 3-13).

FOOT PLACEMENT

A race walker's feet land in an almost exact straight line. After you learn to use your hips efficiently, your foot placement changes slightly to imitate this near straight-line placement. Please beware: when you try to mimic this action without using your hips, you place an undesirable stress across your knee.

Figure 3-15

THE REAR FOOT

Figure 3-16

Many race walkers do not hold their rear foot on the ground long enough. The longer you leave your rear foot on the ground, the more efficient your stride. Leaving the rear foot on the ground longer stretches your hip muscles like a slingshot and the resulting reflex pulls the swing leg forward faster. As the faster-moving swing leg propels your body forward with greater force, you gain even more speed. In addition, your body exerts a force against the ground due to gravity. When you stand still, this force is completely vertical. When you keep the foot on the ground longer, the ground's reactive force of the body's weight becomes more horizontal than vertical when you lift your heel and move to toe off. This force helps to maintain contact with the ground while contributing to forward body propulsion.

FOOT STRIKE

When your foot strikes the ground, land on the back of your heel and point your toes at an angle between 30 and 45 degrees with the ground. Once your foot makes contact, roll it forward, keeping your toes pointed up and off the ground until the entire leg supports your body's weight.

Figure 3-17   *Figure 3-18*   *Figure 3-19*

After heel strike, smooth your stride by rolling onto the midsection of your foot and through to your big toe. Avoid slapping your foot against the ground. If you feel or hear a slap, stop, stretch your shin, and start again.

When you walk with your toes pointed, you use your shin muscles more. How long you keep your toes off the ground is directly related to the strength and flexibility of your shin. However, be aware that holding your toe up upon heel strike may cause a burning sensation in your shins. When you feel this soreness, stop and stretch the shins out using the *Standing Shin Stretch* (chapter 4, page 57) or the *Seated Shin Stretch* (chapter 4, page 58). Slow down a little, walking with pedestrian technique; then, after a few minutes, try the new technique again. The shin pain should go away as you become better conditioned; if it does not, seek assistance from a medical professional.

Proper planting of the foot with a smooth roll through also helps to avoid premature knee bending. Prove it to yourself. Try to land flat-footed with your leg straight. It's not very easy, especially when walking quickly.

Figure 3-20   *Figure 3-21*   *Figure 3-22*

TOE OFF AND A FINAL PUSH

Efficient race walkers do not let their feet lift passively off the ground; instead, just before the rear foot breaks contact with the ground, they actively push the big toe against the ground. If you add this simple flick, you feel a slight float to your stride. Done properly, overall race walking technique becomes less mechanical and movements feel as if they are flowing together in a forward motion. Done improperly, an overly hard push off causes overstriding and flagrant loss of contact with the ground.

Figure 3-23 *Figure 3-24* *Figure 3-25*

Care must be taken to carry your foot forward in a relatively straight line after you push off. When your foot leaves the ground and is swinging forward, try not to twist the foot to the side as your leg progresses. Observe the following figures that demonstrate proper foot carriage.

  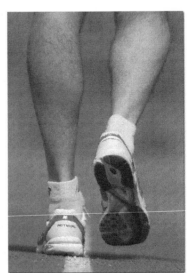

Figure 3-27 *Figure 3-28* *Figure 3-29*

HIPS

Figure 3-30. Denis Nizhegorodov in the 50km at the 2006 World Cup in La Coruña demonstrating excellent forward hip rotation

Elite race walkers generate their primary source of forward locomotion from rotating the hips forward. Repeatedly pivoting the hips forward causes them to act as the body's motor, propelling it forward one step at a time. Actively swinging the hip forward lengthens the stride from the top of the legs, while increasing stride length behind the body. In a flexible race walker, the gain can be as much as six inches per stride. If you add as little as 1 inch to a typical 1-meter race walking stride, the net gain is approximately 10 meters per lap on a track. In a 20km race, that totals to over 500 meters gained. At an elite level, the savings is close to two minutes. In the last three Olympic Games it made the difference between a gold medal and finishing well off the podium.

Look back to Figure 3-2. Notice again how Tallent's stride is distributed more behind the torso than in front of it. This is directly due to hip rotation. Good forward hip rotation is a key solid race walking technique. The value of pursuing increased stride length was illustrated when Tim Seaman trained with Jefferson Perez, the 1996 Olympic champion and 2008 Olympic silver medalist. They measured their stride lengths and found that, while Jefferson is shorter than Tim, Jefferson's stride length was 1.25 meters and Tim's was 1.11 meters. That corresponds to Tim having to take 18,000 steps in a 20km race and Jefferson having to take only 16,000.

Some coaches tout that increasing hip rotation decreases a race walker's cadence. This is an inaccurate evaluation of biomechanics. The hips rotate forward at the same time as the legs swing forward. The leg does not swing forward before the hip rotates. Since the two motions occur simultaneously, any reduction in cadence is minimal and greatly outweighed by the increase in stride length.

The exact motion of the hips during race walking is a bit complicated. The hip moves in three dimensions; its primary movement is forward, but it also must move slightly in and out as well as up and down. To further understand proper technique, observe the following three figures which show the hip motion from varying perspectives.

Imagine a small circular sticker being placed on the outside of the center of the race walker's hip. This sticker represents the center point of the hip in the following figures as the hip moves through four key points of the walker's stride. Figure 3-31 shows the center point of the right hip as a race walker completes one stride when walking on a road or track as viewed from the side.

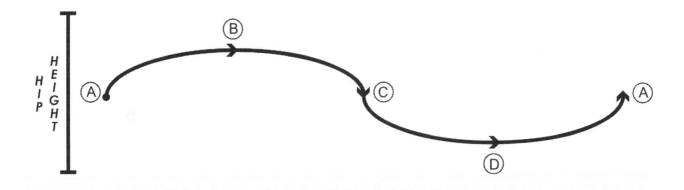

Figure 3-31. View of the hip from the side as a race walker walks on the road

The walker's right heel strikes the ground at (A) as the center point of the hip is in the neutral position. As the body moves forward over a straightened leg, the center point of the hip rises until the straightened leg passes directly beneath the body (B).

From the moment when the leg passes under the body (B) until the right foot's toe pushes off the ground, the center point of the hip moves downwards. As the rear foot swings starts to swing forward (C), the leg must be bent. This bent leg swings forward as the hip continues to lower slightly. This is known as "hip drop" and, while necessary, is a minimal action. After the knee of the swing leg passes under the body (D), the center point of the hip rises to the neutral position (A).

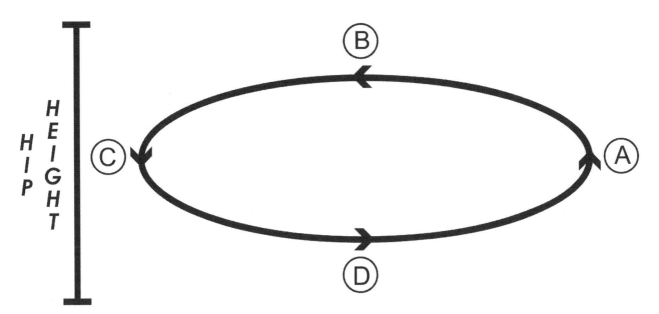

Figure 3-32. View of the hip from the side as a race walker walks on a treadmill

Again, Figure 3-32 shows the center point of the right hip of a race walker's stride as viewed from the side while the race walker is on a treadmill. The walker's heel strikes the ground at (A) as the center point of the hip is in the neutral position. As the treadmill carries the straightened leg backwards, the center point of the hip rises. From the moment when the straightened leg passes under the body (B) until the right foot's toe pushes off the treadmill, the center point of the hip moves down. As the rear foot begins to move forward (C), the leg must be bent. While it does, the hip continues to lower. This is known as "hip drop." After the knee of the swing leg passes under the body (D), the center point of the hip rises to its starting position for heel strike (A).

Finally, to show how the hip arcs out slightly at parts of the stride, observe Figure 3-33. Note that the outward sway is minimal and not a forced action. Instead, the hips sway in or out due to the forces subjected to it by the legs, arms, and torso.

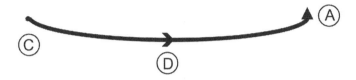

Figure 3-33. View of the hip from the top as a race walker walks on the road

As the walker's right foot is about to leave the ground with the right hip behind the body (C), the right hip begins moving forward. As it does, it arcs out slightly. Once the knee swings under the body (D), the hip continues forward while arcing inward back to the starting position (A).

ARMS AND SHOULDERS

Figure 3-34. Jefferson Perez (1555) showing excellent arm carriage in the 20km at the Beijing Olympic Games

An elite race walker synchronizes arm and hip motion to maximize efficiency and speed. While the exact range of motion for the arm varies slightly with speed and effort, each arm travels from a couple of inches behind the hip to just above the chest line. The primary power for arm movement is derived from the backward swing of your arm. It is not a wild pumping action and does not require much effort to thrust the arm forward. The shoulder acts as a fulcrum with the arms swinging like a pendulum.

With the proper angle, when you drive back, the arm swings to the proper position a few inches behind your hip. With a relaxed shoulder, your arm recoils forward to the correct location. The cycle repeats with another drive of the arm backward. With a relaxed shoulder and proper angle, little effort is required to move your arm backward. Your arms move only as fast as your hips and legs; it's all about synchronicity.

The ratio of upper and lower arm length varies from walker to walker. If you feel you are swinging your arms too far in front of your body, reduce the angle between your upper and lower arms. Similarly, if you have too short an arm swing, increase the angle.

Figure 3-35

Observe Figure 3-35. The length of the arm swing is directly related to the angle between Tim's upper and lower arm. As the angle increases, so does the length of arm swing. If the arm swing is too long, you will overstride, causing too much of your stride to be in front of your body. In contrast, if your arms are too short, the stride is not long enough behind your body. With the proper arm swing, Tim exhibits the proper triangle with his legs.

You can also see how the shoulders and torso move slightly forward as the opposite hip rotates forward. In Figure 3-35 Tim's right shoulder is slightly in front of his left. You can also notice the forward presence of the right side of his torso as it counters the left hip's forward progression.

Proper arm swing must also take into account how the arm crosses in front of the body. Observe Figures 3-36 through 3-38. The arm swings forward as if shaking someone's hand. Moving directly across the body or bringing the arm forward too straight inhibits forward hip rotation.

Figure 3-36

Figure 3-37

Figure 3-38

One key to good arms is to relax the shoulders. While the shoulders do move slightly forward and back, counteracting the forward hip rotation, they should remain relatively still. Many people believe their shoulders are relaxed, but they are not. When we walk, our shoulders often tighten and rise above the desired position. This is like adding friction to the axle of a car.

Observe the height of your shoulders and check whether they are relaxed. Since you won't be carrying a ruler, simply place one hand on your shoulder and lower it as far down as it can go. When your shoulder is all the way down, it is relaxed.

Chapter Four
Legality Issues

If you've race walked competitively long enough, you have probably suffered the dreaded experience of disqualification. Certainly you've picked up a caution or two somewhere along the line. The first thing to realize is that, unless you intentionally tried to violate the rules of race walking, you are not a cheater. In fact, it may be that a judge thought you were not adhering to the definition of race walking while in actuality you were. Most likely, however, the judge's feedback tells you that you need to improve your technique.

Judges' feedback comes in one of three forms: cautions, proposals for disqualification, or actual disqualifications. When a race walking judge believes you are in danger of a violation of the definition, he or she may warn you with a caution paddle. This is not required and serves only as an aid to you during the race. The caution may be for loss of contact with the ground (also known as lifting) or because the knee of the supporting leg is bent at the wrong time. In contrast, the judge may submit a proposal for disqualification (by filling out a red card). If three different judges issue you a red card, then you are disqualified from the race. The notice of disqualification may occur during the race or after the race. This can be done only by the chief judge. This is slightly different in international competition, where a race walker may also be disqualified unilaterally by the chief judge in the final 100 meters of the race.

HOW TO ASSESS IF YOU HAVE A TECHNIQUE PROBLEM

Even if you are a textbook legal walker, with excellent technique, you may receive a caution or two during a race. This is not something to be concerned about and certainly does not mean you should alter your technique. Different judges apply different standards as to when it is appropriate to give a caution. However, in general a caution, without a proposal for disqualification, means that you are close to violating the definition of race walking. While it may not sound right, you **should be** close to violating the definition. As Troy Engle used to say, "Race walking is as close to running as possible, while maintaining the rules of race walking."

In contrast, if you are frequently being disqualified from races or receiving two proposals for disqualification per race, it's time to take a closer look.

While there are many reasons for needing to improve your legality, issues are typically caused by moving faster than your technique allows. From a training perspective, you need to get additional endurance work, while focusing on technique, to build your engine. From a technique perspective, there's a lot more that you can do depending upon your particular legality issue(s). They can be broken into three categories, the last actually not being a cause for disqualification:

1. Loss of contact
2. Knee not straightening
3. Overly legal walking

LOSS OF CONTACT (LIFTING)

Since the 1996 change in the definition of race walking, the determination of whether a race walker loses contact with the ground or not has become more subjective. Because the definition now states that "the walker makes contact with the ground so that no visible (to the human eye) loss of contact occurs," it is now impossible to state definitely whether a race walker is lifting or not. What one human eye perceives, another may not.

At technique clinics, when we first show the following sequence of photographs of elite race walkers, many attendees quickly volunteer that the race walkers are lifting. What do you think? Are they walking with a visible loss of contact? The walker appears to be violating the definition of race walking, because as one enlarges each photograph and examines it closely one can see that both feet are off the ground. However, could the human eye catch that at race speed? It's our opinion that the answer is "not always."

The walkers shown on the following two pages, in our opinion, should not receive proposals for disqualification for loss of contact. While they are off the ground, they certainly are not flagrantly off the ground. An old rule of thumb was that if you are off the ground long enough to be seen for more than one frame in a video camera, then you deserved a red card for lifting. However, today's video cameras are capable of capturing more frames per second. While 24 frames per second used to be the standard, many cameras now capture 30 or even 60 frames per second. There are even cameras capable of an amazing 1000 frames per second, albeit for a very short time.

Therefore, while we can't definitively state that someone is legal or illegal based on a photograph, after taking and analyzing over 150,000 photographs of elite race walkers in the past decade, we recommend some guidelines when looking at images of race walkers. The metric we recommend when looking at still images of race walkers is the combined air under both shoes. If the combined air under both feet is an inch or two, they are totally legal. When they reach about three inches, they are in the danger zone; above that they probably should be disqualified. However, the reality of who gets a disqualification call does not rely solely on the combined height off the ground of a race walker's flight phase. Often it has a lot to do with how good the walker looks, where good is defined as smooth technique. That's why there are so many recommendations in this chapter for improving your technique to avoid lifting.

Are these race walkers lifting? Both are walking in a 50km race, with a cadence of approximately 180-190 steps per minute. Given that they are no more than an inch off the ground with each foot, it is highly unlikely that their loss of contact could be seen by the human eye.

Kamil Kalka, 50km - 2006 World Cup

Jesus Angel Garcia, 50km - 2006 World Cup

Even seen at extreme closeup, these walkers are just barely off the ground and therefore it is our subjective opinion that they are legal.

Kamil Kalka, Extreme Closeup

Jesus Angel Garcia, Extreme Closeup

The next two walkers show a bit more air under their feet. Are they worthy of a red card for lifting? If you look at the close up shots on the following page, it may be your opinion that they should receive a red card. We think it's too close to tell. For what it's worth, neither walker was disqualified from the race.

Trond Nymark, 50km – 2006 World Cup

Salvador Mira, 50km – 2006 World Cup

Trond Nymark, Extreme Closeup

Salvador Mira, Extreme Closeup

These final two walkers, in our humble opinion, are flying high—sky high—and, therefore, should have been disqualified. Sadly, neither walker was removed from the race. It goes to show you the subjectivity of judging the lifting part of the definition of race walking. We have cut the tops of the following two pictures to protect the identity of the athletes. Since they were not disqualified, we do not want to embarrass them or bias the judges in any of their future competitions.

Men's 20km – 2006 World Cup

Women's – 20km – 2006 World Cup

Both photos demonstrate excessive loss of contact.

Men's 20km, Extreme Closeup

Women's 20km, Extreme Closeup

CORRECTING LOSS OF CONTACT (LIFTING)

While it's easy to just say "slow down," there are many aspects of your stride that you can focus on instead of just slowing down. If you can master these changes, then you might not have to slow down much, if at all, to reduce the perception that you are lifting.

FOCUS ON: Quieting the Body Down

While you may not be higher off the ground than the walker next to you, if you have excessive motion throughout your body you may draw the unwanted attention of judges. Bouncing shoulders, bobbing heads, and arms flailing about are all unnecessary. In addition to wasting energy, they can contribute to the perception that you are significantly off the ground. Focus on quieting your body. Try walking in front of a mirror on a treadmill while reducing excessive body motion. Focus on going forward, not up, down, or side to side. The instant feedback received by walking before a mirror goes a long way to improving your form.

FOCUS ON: Lowering your Leg Swing

A big problem for walkers who get calls for lifting is the manner in which they carry their leg as it swings forward. A low foot and knee carriage as the leg swings forward is crucial to efficient technique. It is also crucial to appearing legal. Walkers who gallop forward, driving their knee high, inadvertently drive their foot forward higher off the ground. (See Figures 6-1A & B.) The difference may only be a matter of an inch or two, but that difference appears dramatic to a judge. Focusing on a low vertical position of the foot and knee throughout the leg as it swings forward is one key to reducing your chance of a lifting call.

FOCUS ON: Controling the Range of Motion of Your Arms

Overstriding in front of the body can also lead to lifting. When you reach out too far in front of (or behind) your body, your foot hangs in front of the body, floating for all the judges to see. Often this is caused by swinging your arms too far in front of or behind your body. Focus on good arm carriage and your legs should come back in line. Alternatively, lifting may be caused by reaching forward with your leg instead of your hips. Concentrate on placing the swing leg down shortly after it passes under the torso.

In addition to focusing on the key mental aspects causing lifting, you can also address the physical causes that lead to a visible flight phase. Two of the main offenders are a lack of hip flexor flexibility and tight hamstrings. Practicing the following exercises greatly improves your range of motion and assists in lengthening your stride behind your torso.

BEND DOWN HAMSTRING DRILL

Motivation: We all need to stretch our hamstrings more. Since tight hamstrings make it difficult to maintain a straightened leg once the torso passes over it, a tight hamstring leads to pulling your rear foot off the ground prematurely, resulting in lifting. This exercise is a great way to achieve a better range of motion from your hamstrings, while warming them up before a training walk.

Figure 4-1A

Figure 4-1B

Figure 4-1C

Steps:

A) Standing straight up, place one extended leg six inches in front of your body with toes pointed up.
B) Bend over slowly and, without bending the knee of your extended leg, reach to touch your toes (Figure 4-1A). If you are flexible, try reaching beyond your toes.
C) Walk forward, alternating legs (Figure 4-1B and 4-1C).
D) To relieve the stress on your back, make sure your buttocks is behind your rear foot when touching your toes (Figure 4-1D).
E) Perform this exercise for 30 meters.

Figure 4-1D

LONG STRIDES - LONG ARMS DRILL

Motivation: There are many benefits to this drill. From a perspective of legality, a lack of forward hip rotation has the same effect as tight hamstrings; it leads to your rear foot coming off the group prematurely. This is often due to tight hip flexors. The beauty of this drill is that it increases the range of motion of the hips in a manner specific to race walking.

Sometimes the lack of forward hip rotation in beginner walkers may be due to having difficulty understanding what hip rotation should feel like. The long arm swings help these beginning walkers exaggerate their hips forward with each stride.

Finally, when the body is cold, this is a great way to get blood pumping to all extremities quickly.

Steps:

A) Keeping both arms straight and your hands flat with palms back, race walk with an exaggerated stride by driving your hips forward.
B) Perform this exercise for 30 meters. You should feel a connection between your arms and hips.

Figure 4-2A *Figure 4-2B* *Figure 4-2C*

HURDLERS DRILL

Motivation: As previously stated, forward hip rotation is key to controlling lifting. The *Hurdlers Drill* helps to improve hip and groin flexibility while warming you up for race walking at the same time.

Steps:

A) Lean against a wall or tree (Figure 4-3A).
B) While facing forward, swing your leg forward and up, then back and around, as if it were clearing a hurdle placed at your side (Figures 4-3B through 4-3F).
C) Use a prop such as someone's arm to act as the hurdle if possible.
D) Range of motion is the key to performing this drill correctly. Be sure to extend your leg in as large a circle as possible.
E) Perform this exercise 10-15 times for each leg.

Figure 4-3A

Figure 4-3B

Figure 4-3C

Figure 4-3D

Figure 4-3E

Figure 4-3F

FORWARD LEG KICK DRILL

Motivation: The *Forward Leg Kick Drill* improves the two key areas most often associated with loss of contact: hamstring and hip inflexibility. It does so while warming you up for race walking at the same time.

Steps:

A) Hold onto a pole or tree for balance.
B) Extend your opposite arm and leg as shown in Figure 4-4A.
C) Swing the leg and hip under the body, while bringing the opposite arm back toward the body.
D) Drive the knee up as high as you can, while bringing your opposite arm back behind your body (Figure 4-4B).
E) Reverse your arm and leg swing, extending back to your original position (Figure 4-4A).
F) Repeat this exercise 10-15 times for each leg.

Figure 4-4A

Figure 4-4B

TALES FROM THE TRACK

Four months prior to the 1996 50K Olympic trials, I stepped off a plane in Barcelona where world champion Valenti Massana picked me up at the airport. The first words out of his mouth were, "Welcome to hell." Somehow, I had convinced the Spanish national coach, Jose "Pepe" Marin, to let me come to Spain for two months and train. Thank goodness at that time I thought that Valenti was joking. Otherwise, I would have just gotten back on the plane to go home. Over the next two months I trained harder and longer physically and mentally than ever before. At the end of the two months I was granted permission to compete in the Spanish National 50K. Two weeks prior to the race we had a test week to see just how ready we were for the upcoming race. It is a week I will never forget and will always appreciate.

(Continued on next page)

SIDE LEG SWING DRILL

Motivation: Again our mantra is that forward hip rotation is key to controlling lifting. The *Side Leg Swing Drill* helps to improve hip and groin flexibility while warming you up for race walking at the same time.

Steps:

A) Lean against a pole or tree.
B) Swing your leg up and away from the body, kicking the leg as high as you can (Figure 4-5A).
C) Swing the leg down and in front of the body, letting the hip move across the front of the body (Figure 4-5B).
D) As the leg swings upward in front of your body, extend it as far as your range of motion allows. Lift the heel of your supporting leg off the ground so that you have extra stretch (Figure 4-5C).
E) Reverse your position back to the position in Figure 4-5A.
F) Repeat this exercise 10-15 times for each leg.

Figure 4-5A *Figure 4-5B* *Figure 4-5C*

TALES FROM THE TRACK

(Continued) Monday was 25K in the morning at 5 minutes per kilometer; in the afternoon it was 20 x 400m every 3 minutes with a goal of completing every 400m in 90 seconds and taking a 90-second rest. Tuesday was an easy 3-hour hike in the morning with light jogging and mobility exercises in the afternoon. Wednesday was 50K at 5:30 per kilometer…just slow and easy. Thursday was another easy 2- to 3-hour hike in the morning with light jogging and mobility exercises in the afternoon. Friday was 4 x 10K at goal race pace. At the end of the week, Valenti came up to me and said, "Now you are ready to take the next step in your athletic career." He was right. A week later I raced in the 50K and lowered my PR from 4:19 down to 4:05. Thanks to that training two months later I placed second in my first Olympic trials. Valenti was right…hell it was…but really it was just the path to heaven.

—*Andrew Hermann, U.S. Olympian, 2000 Sydney, Australia*

TRADITIONAL HAMSTRING STRETCH

Motivation: This is an effective seated stretch of the hamstrings and an excellent post-training cool down. By isolating the hamstring muscle specifically, you minimize loss of contact issues.

Steps:

A) Sit down, placing one leg in front of you.
B) Bend your other leg with the sole of your foot facing toward your straight leg and the knee pointed out (Figure 4-6A).
C) Keeping your back straight, lean forward from the hips, reaching towards your toes (Figure 4-6B).
D) Ideally, you should reach past your toes, but remember not to overstretch or bounce while trying to touch them; just stay within your comfort zone.
E) Hold the stretch for 20-30 seconds and repeat 2-3 times with each leg.

Figure 4-6A

Figure 4-6B

EASY ON THE BACK HAMSTRING STRETCH

Motivation: Walkers with really tight hamstrings or lower back problems may wish to start by using this low-stress stretch after warming up.

Figure 4-7

Steps:

A) Lie on the ground and stretch your right leg out.
B) Lift the left leg, holding it as straight as you can (Figure 4-7). The more flexible you are, the closer to your torso you should be able to pull your leg. Take care not to pull your right leg up.
C) Ideally, your leg should be perpendicular to the ground; however, always stretch within your own limits.
D) Hold the stretch for 20-30 seconds and repeat 2-3 times with each leg.

TOE TOUCHING HAMSTRING STRETCH

Motivation: Do you remember being asked to bend over and touch your toes in gym class? Good idea, bad execution. Bending over like that might cause stress to the lower back. Instead, avoid such stress by using the *Toe Touching Hamstring Stretch*.

Steps:

A) Instead of standing straight up, lean against a wall or pole (Figure 4-8A).
B) Keeping your buttocks against the pole, place your feet approximately six inches to one foot away.
C) Continue leaning against the wall while you bend down and try to touch your toes (Figure 4-8B). Focus on preventing your legs from bending. Keeping your feet away from the wall reduces the stress on your back and avoids straining the sciatic nerve, one of the largest nerves in your body, located in the pelvic region.
D) Hold the stretch for 20-30 seconds and repeat 2-3 times.

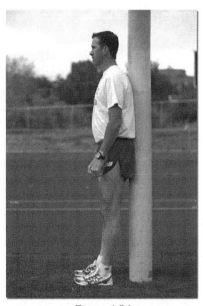
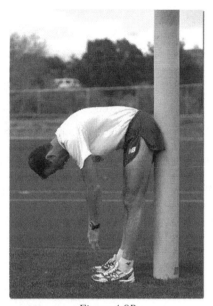

Figure 4-8A   *Figure 4-8B*

TALES FROM THE TRACK

Before I started race walking, I was a fairly decent runner and accustomed to winning races. When I toed the line for a one-mile race walk at the 168th Street Armory in New York City, I had similar expectations of winning. My outlook changed suddenly when the gun went off and the pack blasted away. It was all I could do to hold on for dear life at the back of the pack. Halfway through the race, I remembered thinking this had all the elements of running a race. With my lungs searing, my legs nearing fatigue, and the leaders not too far ahead, I made a decision. Somehow, I would get to the finish line before them. I pressed with all I had and went by them one by one, gaining more momentum; finally I chased and caught the smooth-striding leader. I finished in 7:11 and had no idea if that was a good time or not. *(Continued on next page)*

IMPROVED TOE TOUCHING HAMSTRING STRETCH

Motivation: Sometimes it's not convenient to lean against a wall or sit on the ground when you need to stretch your hamstrings. The *Improved Toe Touching Hamstring Stretch* is almost identical to the *Toe Touching Hamstring Stretch*, although it does not require a wall.

Steps:

   A) To ensure your that buttocks stays far enough behind you to remove the stress from your lower back, cross your feet as depicted in Figure 4-9A.
   B) Bend down and try to touch your toes. Focus on preventing your legs from bending (Figures 4-9B and 4-9C).
   C) Reach as far as you can without causing pain.
   D) Hold the stretch for 20-30 seconds.
   E) Cross your feet in the opposite manner and repeat steps A-D.

Figure 4-9A

Figure 4-9B

Figure 4-9C

TALES FROM THE TRACK

(Continued)

Afterwards, I learned that I had just beaten the National Champion, Susan Liers, and other national-class walkers. I laughed and thought it was a good thing that I was clueless, but I took the lesson to heart and tried never to peg myself in a limited way. I never rest on past performances or think I can't be beaten. So many times I hear athletes, as they arrive at a race, survey the field and decide whom they can't possibly beat. Don't create another opponent in the field. Instead, believe in yourself and race your race.

—*Maryanne Daniel, six-time national champion.*

YOGA STYLE HAMSTRING STRETCH

Motivation: You may be tempted to disregard the exercise below, but this little gem is one of the most rewarding stretches in this book; progressing through it slowly stretches your neck, back, and hamstrings.

Steps:

A) Begin in the same stance as with the *Toe Touching Hamstring Stretch* (Figure 4-10A), then lower just your head, tucking your chin toward your chest (Figure 4-10B).
B) Slowly curl your upper body down and away from the wall.
C) Continue to progress gradually, allowing your hands to drop to your sides (Figure 4-10C).

Figure 4-10A *Figure 4-10B* *Figure 4-10C*

D) Finally, progress through Figures 4-10D to 4-10F, slowly lowering your arms toward your toes. (Touch them if you can.) Try to spend 20 to 30 seconds progressing from Step A to Step D.
E) Finally, hang for another 10 to 20 seconds before reversing the process. Be patient.
F) Reverse the stretch very gradually, concentrating on the sensation of your vertebrae stacking as you progress upwards.

Figure 4-10D *Figure 4-10E* *Figure 4-10F*

LEG UP HAMSTRING STRETCH

Motivation: Sometimes getting down on the ground to stretch your hamstring isn't very convenient. Instead, try stretching your hamstrings standing up.

Steps:
- A) Place your foot on a bench, table, or anything at a comfortable height, while standing far enough back to straighten your leg comfortably (Figure 4-11A).
- B) With a straight back, lean forward, taking care not to bend your knee (Figure 4-11B).
- C) Reach for the toes on your raised foot and hold once you begin to feel the stretch.
- D) Hold the stretch for 20-30 seconds and repeat 2-3 times with each leg.

Figure 4-11A

Figure 4-11B

TALES FROM THE TRACK

Think you have a lot of race walking shoes? Feel like you go through shoes too quickly and then can't find the pair you like anymore? Elite race walkers like Tim Seaman go through 25 pairs of shoes a year. Observe the photo to the left where a small pile of shoes was collected from Tim's high-altitude training camp. The collection was for just four athletes' shoes and a pair of my own from a one-month camp. Imagine how many are piled up in their home!

BENT-KNEE WALKING

Although, according to international judge Ron Daniel, 25 percent of all judges' calls in elite races are for bent knees, in searching through 8,000 photos from the last two Olympics and a World Cup we found only 2 instances of bent-knee race walking. While there may be more cases that the camera didn't capture, the lack of photographic evidence is alarming. Of the elites who were bent-kneed, one case was at a water stop and the other around a turn.

The story is different with masters race walkers and beginners. People come to race walking from a variety of backgrounds, but virtually none of them require, in daily life, that they walk with a straightened knee or the toe pointed as it is at a race walker's heel strike. Therefore, at first straightening the knee at heel strike and maintaining a straightened knee until the leg passes under the body may prove difficult. It takes a while to train the knee to maintain a straightened leg. Don't despair, though; there are many corrective actions you can take to straighten up!

CORRECTING BENT-KNEE ISSUES

The bad news is that bent knee issues are one of the hardest problems to correct for a race walker. The good news is that almost anyone can correct them. Sure, you'll hear people say "my leg just doesn't straighten," but what they really mean is that it can't straighten at the pace they wish to walk. So the first advice is to slow down and walk within the limits of your technique.

> ### FOCUS ON: Keeping Your Toe Up at Landing
>
> Try landing flatfooted and keeping your leg straightened as your weight is supported by the leg. It's not easy to do, especially if your foot lands any reasonable distance in front of your torso. While most people do not land flatfooted when they race walk, you may be like many who land with the toe pointed, but then flatten the foot too quickly. Therefore, try to focus on keeping the toes of your foot pointed up as your heel strikes the ground. Then, as your torso comes forward over the supporting leg, roll through the foot, gradually lowering the toes to a flatfooted position. A simple check is to listen for your toes slapping into the ground. If you hear them, you are not holding them up long enough.

FOCUS ON: Shortening Your Stride in Front

Bent-knee walking is often caused by striking the ground too far in front of the body. If you are overstriding while you walk, you may actually land with a straightened knee. However, as your torso moves forward, the bulk of your body's weight is loaded onto the supporting leg and the knee begins to bend. As it does, the quadriceps muscles fire, attempting to straighten your leg. If you focus on a shorter stride in front of your body, your leg supports less weight and it is easier for you to keep the knee straightened.

FOCUS ON: Good Hip Rotation

One key to landing and maintaining a straightened knee is to have a shorter stride in front of the body and a longer stride behind the body. The key to achieving this ratio is proper hip rotation. Focus on driving the hips forward with each stride. Minimize side-to-side hip movement as well as any unnecessary hip drop.

Concentration alone will probably not be enough to correct bent-knee race walking. Strengthening the muscles used to straighten the leg and improving the flexibility of your hips, hamstrings, shins, and calves greatly assist walking with proper legal technique.

ISOMETRIC KNEE EXERCISES

Motivation: This mild strength training exercise requires no extra weight and minimal movement of your body. It's isometric and trains your muscle memory to know what it feels like to straighten the knee.

Steps:

A) Wrap a towel under your legs (Figure 4-12A).
B) Press down on the towel, straightening your knee (Figure 4-12B).
C) Hold for 3 seconds.
D) Repeat steps B and C 10-15 times.

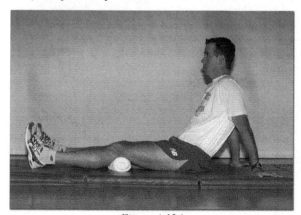

Figure 4-12A

Figure 4-12B

STRAIGHT LEG RAISE EXERCISE

Motivation: Like the isometric exercise shown earlier, this exercise strengthens the quadriceps, but it also strengthens the hip flexors and abdominals. Since it strengthens your leg while keeping it straightened, it helps to promote muscle memory that enables you to walk without bending your knees at the incorrect time.

This exercise can be done with or without a light ankle weight. Start without weight and gradually add light weights, building up to but never exceeding 10 percent of your body weight.

Steps:

A) Start by lying on your back and supporting your body by bending one leg as shown in Figure 4-13A.
B) Slowly raise the other straightened leg to about 45 degrees (Figure 4-13B); hold it there for a second, and then gradually lower it.
C) Repeat this exercise 15 times with one leg, then switch and repeat with the other leg.

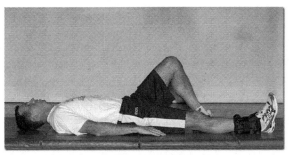
Figure 4-13A

Figure 4-13B

WRITE THE ALPHABET EXERCISE

Motivation: Strengthening and stretching the minor muscles around the ankle can really help with your heel plant, roll through, and push off. When your lower leg muscles aren't strong enough, either you will land flatfooted or your foot will flatten very quickly. If your foot is flat on the ground while it is still in front of your torso, your risk of a bent knee call is high.

Steps:

A) Sit down on a chair.
B) Place one leg over the other.
C) Slowly spell each letter of the alphabet with your toe.
D) Repeat with the other leg.

Options: If you have a light ankle weight, you can place it around your foot and add extra resistance. This resistance could also be accomplished using an elastic band.

SLOW WALKING WITH HEEL PLANT DRILL

Motivation: The old adage of "take baby steps" is also true for race walking drills. Walking slowly with an exaggerated heel plant is a superb way to practice landing with a straightened knee without the pressure of going fast. This drill also allows you to develop the feel for proper foot roll.

Steps:

- A) Using legal race walking technique, start by taking a short step, emphasizing the toe up and straightened knee (Figure 4-14A).
- B) Roll through the stride, keeping the supporting foot's toes off the ground as long as possible (Figure 4-14B).
- C) Place the swing leg's foot down directly in front of the body, again emphasizing the toe up and straightened knee (Figure 4-14C).
- D) Repeat for 30 meters.

Figure 4-14A   *Figure 4-14B*   *Figure 4-14C*

FOOT PLANT DRILL

Motivation: By rocking back and forth while practicing your foot plant, you can train your body to straighten your knee upon foot strike.

Steps:

A) Stand with your weight on both legs. Your lead foot is directly in front of your body, as if you are getting ready to walk in a straight line (Figure 4-15A).
B) Switch your weight to the left leg and begin to swing forward with your right leg.
C) Your left knee is now straightened and supports all your weight. Your right leg is swinging through with your toe and foot as low to the ground as possible. Notice that the right knee is not driving forward and that the next movement is basically only the lower part of the right leg swinging forward (Figure 4-15B).
D) Your right lower leg swings forward with the upper part of the leg moving very little. As the right foot strikes the ground, your weight transfers from the left leg to the right leg (Figure 4-15C).
E) Do not continue to walk forward; rather, step back to the position shown in Figure 4-15A.
F) Repeat steps A-D 10-15 times with the left leg, then switch and repeat it 10-15 times with the right leg.

Figure 4-15A

Figure 4-15B

Figure 4-15C

WALK ON YOUR HEELS EXERCISE

Motivation: The single biggest physical cause of bent-knee walking is a lack of adequate shin strength to allow the foot to land with the toe pointed and properly roll through toe off. The single easiest way to strengthen your shins is to walk on your heels.

Steps

A) Walk slowly, with a stride of no more than six inches. Remember, it's not a race.
B) Focus on how high you point your toes. The higher you point them, the better and more intensely you work your shins.
C) Maintain this technique for 30 meters.

Figure 4-16A

Figure 4-16B

If your shins can't handle this distance, stop walking on your heels briefly and stretch out your shins. Once you have stretched properly, resume heel-walking the remainder of the 30 meters. Upon completion, always stretch out the shins (See chapter 4, page 57) completely; you will feel happy that you did so later.

TOE RAISE EXERCISE

Motivation: This is another good shin strengthening exercise to help you land with your toe pointed and roll through to toe off.

Perform this more advanced shin exercise on the edge of a curb or step. Because balance is sometimes difficult when performing this exercise, make sure that you have a pole or wall to steady yourself.

Steps:

A) Facing away from the curb/step, place your heels as close to the edge as possible, taking care to remain steady.
B) Pump your toes up and down as quickly as possible (Figures 4-17A and 4-17B).
C) Get those toes up high and low! The greater the range of motion your toes pass through, the better the workout.

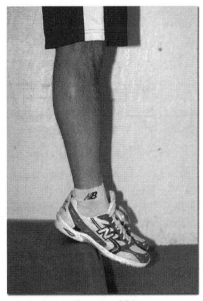 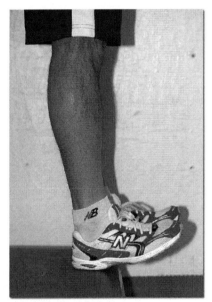

Figure 4-17A *Figure 4-17B*

Upon completion, always stretch out the shins (See chapter 4, page 57) completely.

Caution: Please be cautious. The shin muscles are very small and easily irritated. If you overdo this exercise, the shin muscles will become tight and fatigued, making it difficult to race walk properly.

WALK ON YOUR TOES EXERCISE

Motivation: Strengthening muscles involves balance. While athletes often focus on their shins to correct bent-knee walking, they neglect their complementary muscles, the calves. This exercise is similar to the shin strengthening exercise *Walk on Your Heels*. However, by slowly walking on your toes, you strengthen your calves.

Steps:

A) Walk slowly, with a stride of no more than six inches. Remember, it's not a race.
B) As you walk, focus on keeping your heels as high off the ground as possible.
C) Walk this way for about 30 meters.

If your calves tire quickly, stop walking on your toes briefly and stretch your calves a little. Then complete the rest of the exercise. If walking 30 meters feels really easy, try to go a little further.

Once you finish the exercise, it's always a good idea to stretch the calves completely as shown later in this chapter.

Figure 4-18A

Figure 4-18B

Figure 4-18C

CALF RAISE EXERCISE

Motivation: The *Calf Raise* exercise also strengthens the calf muscles, which balance the shin strengthening exercises. In addition, by doing so, you enable yourself to push off more easily and with greater force.

This exercise is best executed with something nearby to help you maintain your balance. Ideally, practice the calf raise on a curb near a pole or on a step with a handrail.

Steps:

A) Find a step or curb and position your toes as close to the edge as possible while still maintaining balance.
B) Place both of your heels beyond the edge, raising and lowering them through a wide range of motion (Figures 4-19A and 4-19B).
C) Repeat this motion 10 to 15 times, taking care not to cheat by using your upper body for leverage.
D) If you are strong enough, try raising and lowering your body on one foot at a time (Figure 4-19C).

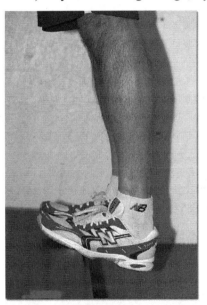
Figure 4-19A

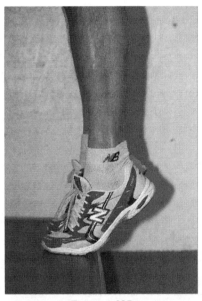
Figure 4-19B

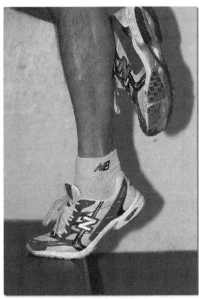
Figure 4-19C

TALES FROM THE TRACK

Training throughout the 2004 season was awesome. I trained all year with Tim Seaman and Kevin Eastler in a great team atmosphere that directly led to the three of us achieving the "A" standard and qualifying to represent our countries in the Olympics. Then disaster struck. I was informed that I had mononucleosis on the very day when I was supposed to leave for the Olympics. The disappointment was crushing. Unable to join my teammates for my first Olympics, I felt the pressure of my sister's Olympic silver medal weighing down upon me. For the next four years, I had that burden upon my shoulder of having missed Athens, but once I qualified for Beijing, everything seemed to come together.
(Continued on next page)

LEG EXTENSION WITH MACHINE EXERCISE

Motivation: Strong quadriceps are essential for race walking. The quadriceps help the lower leg to swing forward as quickly as possible and are directly responsible for helping to straighten the knee. The goal is to make this muscle strong, but not too big, as a big quadriceps hampers our efficiency. Therefore, we want to use low weights and a high number of repetitions to get the muscle in its optimal form for race walking.

Ideally, perform this exercise on a machine, one leg at a time. While machine models differ, most are similar in structure to the one shown below. Higher-quality machines usually allow you to adjust the seat and leg roller. Set the equipment so that your knee is on the axis of the machine, with your ankle just below the leg roller (Figure 4-20A).

Steps:

A) Keeping your shin pressed against the machine, extend your leg to near locking position (Figure 4-20B).
B) Lower your leg to its original position.
C) Repeat this exercise 10-15 times with each leg for 2-3 sets.

Figure 4-20A

Figure 4-20B

Note: Remember to exhale as you raise the leg roller and inhale as you lower it. As you execute the exercise, make sure that your ankle remains in contact with the roller and that you are controlling the weight.

TALES FROM THE TRACK

(Continued)

I watched the opening ceremonies from my hotel outside of Beijing, knowing that I would be able to hear the roar of the crowd at the start of the 20km walk 7 days later. Unfortunately, the race didn't go well. I finished a disappointing 21st. However, with the 50K just 6 days later, I was able to refocus. This time things went according to plan and I regrouped with a 5th place finish in a time of 3:45:08. While I was utterly exhausted, the joy of proving to myself that the 20km was just a bad day at the office and the knowledge that I was one of the best in the world more than made up for it. So keep persevering and never give up on your dreams. My current dream is an Olympic medal in the 2012 London games.

—*Erik Tysse, two-time Olympian from Norway and 5th place at the 2008 Beijing Olympics 50K.*

LEG EXTENSION WITHOUT MACHINE EXERCISE

Motivation: We know quadriceps strength is important, but some of us may not have a leg extension machine accessible. Here's a low-tech way to achieve the same results.

Steps:

A) Sit in a tall stool or chair.
B) Strap a light ankle weight around your ankle.
C) Straighten the leg with the ankle weight.
D) Lower the leg, while exhaling, to the original position.
E) Repeat 15 times and then switch legs.
F) Repeat for 3 sets.

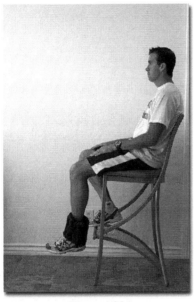

Figure 4-21A

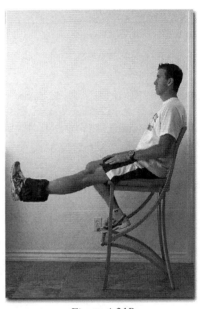

Figure 4-21B

TALES FROM THE TRACK

I will never forget the workout that we did on March 9, 1999. It was two days after Curt Clausen and I had a "gold medal" weekend. I walked 25km on Saturday and Curt completed 30km at American record paces. The next day we did an official race on the track at the ARCO training center. I broke the American record for 3,000m in a time of 11:19.2 and Curt broke the U.S. record for the 5km. Two days later our training partner, Jefferson Perez, had a 5 x 3km workout. Jefferson completed his fourth interval in about 11:30. He then looked over at me and asked very seriously, "What is the track record for 3km?" I thought for a second and smiled. I knew what he was going to do. I told him it was 11:19. He smiled back and started his last interval. Like clockwork, Jefferson reeled off splits of 1:30 per lap, eventually finishing in 11:17 to unofficially take away my track record. Thankfully, he is not American.

—*Tim Seaman, two-time Olympian*

LEG CURL WITH MACHINE EXERCISE

Motivation: Strong hamstrings are important to race walking. The hamstrings are active during every phase of a race walker's stride. Sometimes they are eccentrically contracting (tensing the muscle as it lengthens); at other times they are concentrically contracted (tensing the muscle as it shortens). Either way, it is imperative that we keep them strong to maximize their efficiency and our legality.

This exercise is best performed on a machine, one leg at a time. With few exceptions, most machines are similar in structure to the one shown below. Higher-quality equipment usually allows you to adjust the seat and leg roller; set them so that you situate your knee on the axis of the machine, with the ankle just below the leg roller.

Steps:

A) Keeping your thigh pressed against the machine, curl your leg, pulling your heels inward so that the leg roller approaches your buttocks as shown in Figures 4-22A and 4-22B.
B) Remember to exhale as you raise the weight.
C) Complete the exercise by lowering your leg back to its original position while inhaling.
D) Always maintain contact between the roller and your leg as you execute the lift, as well as maintaining control of the weight.
E) Repeat 10-15 times with each leg and complete 3 sets.

Figure 4-22A

Figure 4-22B

LEG CURL WITHOUT MACHINE EXERCISE

Motivation: We know hamstring strength is important, but some of us may not have a leg curl machine accessible. Here's a low-tech way to achieve the same results using an ankle weight to simulate the machine.

Steps:

- A) Stand next to a wall or pole for balance.
- B) Strap a light ankle weight around your ankle (Figure 4-23A).
- C) Raise the leg with the ankle weight, while inhaling, so that your lower leg is parallel with the floor. Support yourself with the opposite leg (Figure 4-23B).
- D) Hold for one second.
- E) Lower the leg, while exhaling, to the original position.
- F) Repeat 15 times and then switch legs.
- G) Repeat for 3 sets.

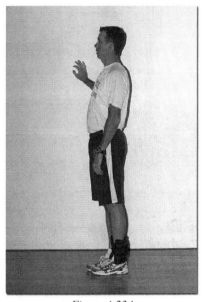

Figure 4-23A

Figure 4-23B

TRADITIONAL CALF STRETCH

Motivation: If your calves are tight, it is difficult to point your toe and straighten your knee at heel strike.

Figure 4-24

Steps:

A) Place both hands at shoulder height on a wall or pole in front of your body.
B) Keep your arms fairly straight and your lead leg bent under your body.
C) Place the heel of your rear leg 1½ to 2 feet behind your body.
D) Keeping your rear leg fairly straight but not locked in position, place the heel of this foot on the ground.
E) You should feel a stretch down the outer part of your rear-leg calf muscle. If you don't, try moving your rear foot back a little farther (remember to place your heel back on the ground after you move your foot back).
F) Throughout the stretch, your upper body should remain vertical and straight; do not bend forward.
G) Alternate legs when finished.

BENT KNEE CALF STRETCH

Motivation: The calf is not a single muscle; it comprises two muscles, both of which need stretching. The previous stretch worked the outer calf muscle. The *Bent Knee Calf Stretch* may not feel effective initially, but it utilizes an excellent position that stretches deep in the inner calf muscle. You can start this stretch as you finish the *Traditional Calf Stretch*.

Figure 4-25

Steps:

A) Place both hands, shoulder high, on a pole or wall in front of your body.
B) Keep your arms fairly straight with one leg slightly bent under your body.
C) Place the heel of your rear leg 1 to 1 ½ feet behind your body. Notice that this is about six inches in front of the placement for the *Traditional Calf Stretch*.
D) Keeping your rear leg fairly straight and in a stable position, place the heel of your rear foot on the ground.
E) Now, keeping your heel planted, bend the rear leg so that your knee drops a few inches closer to the ground. You should feel a deeper but less pronounced stretch in your calf muscle. While not as pronounced as the other stretches, this one definitely works on the targeted muscle.

ADVANCED CALF STRETCH

Motivation: If your calves are extremely flexible, you may want a deeper stretch. Try the *Advanced Calf Stretch*. Because this stretch is relatively aggressive, you may need to build up to it by practicing the *Traditional Calf Stretch* first. The more flexible your calf muscles are, the better foot plant and roll you will achieve.

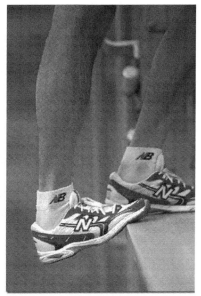

Figure 4-26

Steps:

A) Place one foot as close as possible to the edge of a step or curb while maintaining good balance. If possible, use a tree, pole, or even another walker for balance.

B) While keeping your rear leg as straight as possible, lower your heel over the curb as far as it will go comfortably. You'll achieve the best stretch by hanging as close to the edge as possible and lowering your heels as far as they will go.

C) After holding the stretch for 20-30 seconds, alternate legs.

If you still feel tight, repeat this stretch more than once.

INTENSIVE CALF STRETCH

Motivation: The following stretch is the most aggressive calf stretch included. We use it to stretch the upper areas of the calf that are not reached by less intensive stretching. Be sure to use care when first executing this stretch as you can easily overextend your calf if you bounce or move into this position too forcefully. Unlike the first two calf stretches, the advanced stretch concentrates on the muscles of your upper calf. You may want to work up to this position by practicing the other stretches for a few weeks first.

Steps:

A) Once again, you will need a wall or pole for support.
B) Following Tim's example, begin by standing about an arm's length away from the pole (Figure 4-27). (The closer to the pole you stand, the more you stretch the calf.)
C) Place the heel of the first leg close to the bottom of the pole with the toes against it, as if you were trying to step on the pole.
D) Now keep your leg and back straight and lean into the wall slowly.
E) Being careful not to reach the point of pain, lean into your front leg until you feel moderate tension in your upper calf. Hold the stretch for 20 to 30 seconds, then alternate legs.

Figure 4-27

STANDING SHIN STRETCH

Motivation: All race walkers will tell you that their shins take a real beating from race walking, and when your shins are sore it becomes difficult to land with the toe pointed. Therefore, we must treat our shins kindly. If you don't, you'll surely develop shin splints and know firsthand how this tiny little muscle can cause big problems. The *Standing Shin Stretch* is just one way to take care of it. However, be careful not to overdo it; otherwise the shin muscle will get back at you on your next walk.

Steps:
- A) Balance yourself near a pole or wall.
- B) Put your weight on the supporting leg (Figure 4-28A).
- C) Now touch the other foot to the ground, toe first, and pull your rear foot forward just to the point where it is about to move forward (Figure 4-28B).
- D) Hold it there. You should feel the shin muscles elongate and loosen up.

Do not rest on your big toe as shown in Figure 4-28C.

Figure 4-28A

Figure 4-28B

Figure 4-28C

SEATED SHIN STRETCH

Motivation: The *Seated Shin Stretch* is an effective stretch but has drawbacks. For one thing, you must sit on the ground. If you are in the middle of a race, this is particularly inconvenient. The other problem is that you need grass to perform the stretch, or some very tough knees. Nevertheless, this stretch is very effective in loosening overworked shins and enables you to point your toe and roll through properly.

Steps:

A) Sit on the grass or soft carpet with your legs folded directly under your thighs. See Figures 4-29A and 4-29B; note that the shoelaces touch the ground.
B) Use one hand to support your weight and the other to lift your knee.
C) This lifting should send a stretch down your shin.
D) Hold it 20 to 30 seconds, and then switch legs.

Figure 4-29A

Figure 4-29B

BACK OF KNEE STRETCH

Motivation: Sometimes a pain creeps up on you out of nowhere, as with pain behind the knee. Race walking sometimes aggravates this area, and it sneaks up so slowly that you don't actually realize it until it's too late. With a pain behind the knee, it is very difficult to straighten the knee properly. Avoid this potentially painful problem by adding the stretch below to your warm-down routine.

Steps:

A) In a seated position, place one leg straight in front of you.
B) Bend the knee of the non-stretching leg, placing the foot on the inside of the opposite thigh, forming a triangle.
C) Keeping a straight back, bend from the hips and lean toward your toe.
D) If your hamstring flexibility allows, pull your toes towards your body as shown in Figure 4-30A.
E) If you lack flexibility in the hamstrings and are not able to reach your toes, use a towel, as shown in Figure 4-30B, to extend your reach and get cracking on those hamstrings!

Figure 4-30A

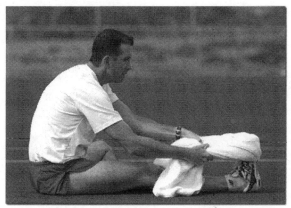

Figure 4-30B

BEND DOWN HAMSTRING DRILL

Motivation: The hamstrings are active during every phase of a race walker's stride. Sometimes they are eccentrically contracting; at other times they are concentrically contracted. Either way, it is imperative that we keep them flexible to maximize their efficiency.

See chapter 4, page 32 for steps to complete this drill.

TRADITIONAL HAMSTRING STRETCH

Motivation: Hamstring flexibility is a key to efficient race walking technique.

See chapter 4, page 37 for steps to complete this drill.

LEG UP HAMSTRING STRETCH

Motivation: Hamstring flexibility is a key to efficient race walking technique.

See chapter 4, page 41 for steps to complete this drill.

 ## LONG STRIDES - LONG ARMS DRILL

Motivation: An improvement in forward hip rotation is likely to improve your ability to straighten the knee on impact and keep it straightened until your leg passes the vertical position. When your hips rotate forward, the amount of your stride in front of your torso is reduced, thus reducing the likelihood that your leg will bend as you ride forward on it. Therefore, this and any other drills that target improved forward hip rotation are very useful to avoid bent-knee issues.

See chapter 4, page 33 for steps to complete this drill as well as the drills in chapter 5, starting on page 67.

BEING OVERLY LEGAL

Ray Sharp early in the race at the 50km 2006 World Cup walking with a minimal if any double support phase.

Ray Sharp, later in the race, showing a significant double support phase.

While not a cause for disqualification, being too legal is not desirable either. Having too long of a double support phase (i.e., both feet are on the ground at the same time) is highly inefficient and slows you down. Elite walkers, unless they have hit the wall, walk with no or a very minimal double support phase. A smooth transition from the rear foot pushing off the ground to riding over the lead leg is a must. If both your front foot and rear foot are in contact with the ground for an extended duration, then while your rear foot is pushing off to propel you forward, its force is counterbalanced by the braking action of your forward foot. One sees an excessive double support phase in beginning walkers who have yet to develop the muscles and flexibility to walk properly or with older walkers who share similar deficiencies.

FOCUS ON: Turnover

One simple way to reduce your double support time is to increase your cadence by picking up and putting down your feet more quickly.

FOCUS ON: Pushing off the Rear Foot

Put a little oomph in your stride with a flick off your big toe. By pushing off your big toe, when your foot is behind the torso, you drive your body forward with more force. The additional force helps to reduce your double support phase. However, be careful: if you push off prematurely, your body is pushed upward instead of forward.

FOCUS ON: Forward Hip Rotation

We can't say enough times that it's all in the hips. Rotating your hips effectively lengthens your stride behind your body. One reason why people overstride is that they are trying to achieve a longer stride length. However, by reaching in front of the body with the leg, you are not propelling your body forward. In actuality, you are slowing your progress. On the other hand, if your stride length increases due to good forward hip rotation, the increase in your stride is behind the body, where it can help to propel you forward.

FOCUS ON: Training

Training can improve your style if you lack leg speed or are overweight. If you lack leg speed, add a rhythm or economy workout once a week. One of our favorites is Bohdan Bulakowski's rhythm workout of 100-, 200-, 300-meter sets with 100 meters of walking easy in between. This is a great workout to get you on your toes with your legs moving quickly.

If you have some extra pounds to lose, getting rid of them helps to get you up on your feet more. Easy distance walking is best for weight loss, so if you have a weight issue, reduce the intensity of your workouts and increase the distance. Don't fret; you can still work on speed as you lose weight by adding a few 30-second pickups at the end of your workout. Later, when you've reached your weight loss goal, add the intensity back in gradually.

QUICK STEPS - HANDS BEHIND BACK DRILL

Motivation: All *Quick Step* drills help to increase your speed, increase your turnover rate, and reduce overstriding. In addition, this *Quick Step* drill allows you to practice getting your toes up. It also forces you to straighten your knee as quickly as possible. Furthermore, when you place your hands behind your back the hips are forced to move without the aid of the arms pumping forward and back, thus helping you develop forward hip rotation. Race walking competitively is about technique and speed, even for the 50km. Italy's Alex Schwazer averaged under 21:45 each 5km to take the home the gold in Beijing.

Steps:

    A) Race walk with normal leg technique, but place the hands behind the back and walk with very short strides (12 inches or less).
    B) Focus on quieting your shoulders and torso.
    C) Focus on turnover, forcing your feet to pick up and come down very quickly.
    D) Focus on planting with your heel, landing with your toe up, and rolling through smoothly.

Figure 4-31A   *Figure 4-31B*   *Figure 4-31C*

QUICK STEPS - HANDS BEHIND HEAD DRILL

Motivation: All *Quick Step* drills help to increase your speed, increase your turnover rate, and reduce overstriding. In addition, when you place your hands behind your head, your hips are forced to move without the aid of the arms pumping forward and back, thus helping you develop better hip rotation.

Steps:

A) Race walk with normal leg technique, but place the hands behind the head and walk with very short strides (12 inches or less).
B) Focus on quieting your shoulders and torso.
C) Focus on turnover, forcing your feet to pick up and place down very quickly.
D) Focus on planting with your heel, landing with your toe up, and rolling through smoothly.

Figure 4-32A　　　　　*Figure 4-32B*　　　　　*Figure 4-32C*

QUICK STEPS SUPERMAN DRILL

Motivation: All *Quick Step* drills help to increase your speed, increase your turnover rate, and reduce overstriding. In addition, as you place your hands out in front of your body, your head is held as flat as possible. Excessive movement of the head could cause judges to think that you are lifting. Therefore, this is good practice not only for our feet, but also for our head.

Steps:

A) Race walk with normal leg technique, but place your hands in front of your body and walk with very short quick strides (12 inches or less).
B) Focus on quieting your shoulders and torso.
C) Focus on turnover, forcing your feet to pick up and come down very quickly.
D) Focus on planting with your heel, landing with your toe up, and rolling through smoothly.

Figure 4-33A   *Figure 4-33B*   *Figure 4-33C*

TALES FROM THE TRACK

Once upon a time, at the start of the Norwegian championships, the weather was schizophrenic. The day started with sunshine and strong winds, but then the weather reversed itself and the rain came on hard just as the winds died down. Given the conditions, I couldn't imagine a good result for the day's races. Unfortunately, there was plenty of time to worry about it, as the men's 20km started at 3pm, while our 10km start was a half an hour later. Amazingly, five minutes before the race started the rain stopped and we had perfect conditions: no sun, 60 degrees F, and almost no winds. You couldn't ask for it any better for long distance race walking. The men's race started really fast with Trond Nymark and my brother Erik passing 5km in 20:28.

(Continued on next page)

QUICK STEPS AIRPLANE DRILL

Motivation: All *Quick Step* drills help to increase your speed, increase your turnover rate, and reduce overstriding. In addition, as you place your hands out to your sides, the hips are forced to move without the aid of the arms pumping forward and back, thus helping you to develop better hip rotation.

Steps:

- A) Race walk with normal leg technique, but place your hands out to the sides of your body and walk with very short quick strides (12 inches or less).
- B) Focus on quieting your shoulders and torso.
- C) Focus on turnover, forcing your feet to pick up and come down very quickly.
- D) Focus on planting with your heel, landing with your toe up, and rolling through smoothly.

Figure 4-34A   Figure 4-34B   Figure 4-34C

TALES FROM THE TRACK

(Continued) We started only 50m in front of them as they were about to pass 7km. With my brother hot on my heels, I didn't think about times at all. I was just walking for my life! Erik pushed even harder and walked the next 5km in 20:18. Already at 3km I felt that this would be hard, but I kept on fighting and talked myself into that it was only 2km until 5km. Passing 5km in 20:25, I found a new goal in not letting Erik pass me before he completed 15km. While I didn't make it, as Erik passed me at around 7.5km, the fantastic competition pushed me even harder. I wasn't aware of how fast I was going. I was only fighting, fighting, fighting the whole way! When I crossed the line, someone told me "41:16." Then the tears poured out. How did I walk this fast? 41:16 was #2 on the all-time world list and a Nordic best performance. My crying was not done for the day as only 12 minutes later my brother Erik won the Norwegian Championship in 1:22:29. I was so proud of him. It was a double victory day and one I will never forget.

—Kjersti Plätzer, 2000 and 2008 20km Walk Olympic silver medalist

HELP SUPPORT AMERICA'S RACE WALKERS

The **North American Race Walking Institute** (NARI) is a nonprofit corporation solely concerned with the promotion of fitness and competitive race walking. The Institute was founded by Elaine Ward under the sponsorship of the North American Race Walking Foundation in 1992. In November 2007, Tom Eastler and A.C. Jaime assumed responsibility for the Institute to insure the continuance of its many successful programs.

The North American Race Walking Institute (NARI) is funded by the tax-deductible donations of individuals and businesses as well as by grants from charitable foundations. The Officers and Board of Directors of the Institute serve as volunteers so that all donations go directly to the development of promising youth and collegiate athletes with the goal of international and Olympic competition.

Donors of $25 or more receive a tax-deductible receipt as well as bulletins with news of the U.S. athletes and their upcoming races. The bulletin also includes championship races, training and health tips. For donations, make checks payable to **NARI** and mail them to either of the following persons.

A.C. Jaime
621 N. 10th Street, Suite C
McAllen, TX 78501-4513
(956) 686-2337
acjaime@sbcglobal.net

Tom Eastler
300 Mosher Hill Road
Farmington, ME 04938
(207) 778-6703
eastler@maine.edu

THE AL HEPPNER MEMORIAL FUND

In honor of Al Heppner, an outstanding walker, journalist, and person, an annual award will be made from the Al Heppner Memorial Fund to young walkers who best meet the qualifications set by the Fund's protocol. Set up as an endowment fund, it provides a permanent vehicle for members of the race walking community to aid young race walkers.

Past Recipients
2008 - Lauren Forgues, University of Phoenix

2008 - Chris Tegtmeier, Concordia University, Nebraska

Chapter Five
Hip Issues

Hips are the primary motor driving your body forward. Therefore, race walking can be incredibly frustrating to beginning walkers who cannot seem to get the feel of proper hip motion. Saying "use your hips more" just falls upon deaf ears. Walkers with minimal hip motion need drills and exercises to help them learn. Other race walkers may have hip motion, but in all the wrong directions. This chapter demonstrates how to correct both problems.

CORRECTING MINIMAL FORWARD HIP ROTATION

When race walkers do not have enough forward hip rotation, it may be because they don't understand what to do, or because their hip muscles are too tight and resist the necessary motion. The first group of walkers usually just needs to feel the hips rotating properly once in order to get a mental image of good forward hip rotation. After that, they can practice driving the hips forward on each stride. The problem may also be due to poor posture, because leaning forward or backward restricts forward hip rotation. In addition, even walkers who have the feel of forward hip rotation may still need to work on their hips' range of motion to maximize stride efficiency. Therefore, if you do not grasp the proper hip rotation, try the first three exercises: *Vampire on the Hill*, *Gunslinger*, and *Long Arms*. If your problem is posture, see chapter 8. Finally, anyone needing to increase forward hip rotation should work on the rest of the drills in this chapter to increase hip flexibility.

Good hip rotation

Minimal hip rotation

Antonio Pereir (left) demonstrating improper posture and minimal forward hip rotation, with the result that he has having too much of his stride in front of his body. In contrast, Erik Tysse (right) demonstrates proper posture and the proper stride ratio.

VAMPIRE ON A HILL EXERCISE

Motivation: If you are having difficulty feeling the proper motion of the hips, try this drill to help you feel their forward rotation.

Figure 5-1

Steps:

A) Stand at the base of a relatively steep hill that is steep enough to be difficult, but not so steep that you cannot maintain legal race walking technique as you walk up it.
B) Place your arms across your chest (as a vampire places his arms when he is in a coffin; see Figure 5-1).
C) Start to race walk up the hill.
D) Feel the tugging of your hips, due to the lack of counterbalance from your arms.
E) After 10-20 yards exaggerate that feeling in the hips.
F) Continue to walk another 10-20 yards, exaggerating the hip drive forward.
G) Continue the exaggeration, but now use your arms as you normally would while race walking.

You should feel a more powerful hip rotation.

GUNSLINGER EXERCISE

Motivation: This drill doesn't work for everyone, but if the *Vampire on a Hill Exercise* doesn't help you feel forward hip rotation, try this one.

Steps:

A) Imagine that you are standing in front of a pair of saloon doors with a gap in front of them almost as wide as your hips.
B) Imagine walking through the doors, with a gun holstered on each hip.
C) Push the saloon door open by thrusting each hip forward so the gun would hit the door and pop it forward.

FUNKY HIP DRILL

Motivation: The *Funky Hip Drill* stretches the hip in a manner consistent with race walking technique. This improves the fluidity of the hip motion.

Steps:

A) Stand in the double support phase, with your right leg forward and your arms behind your back (Figure 5-2A).
B) Raise the toes of your right foot, like when you plant your heel in race walking.
C) Shift your weight to your right leg. Make sure that your right leg is straightened.
D) Push your right hip to the outside (Figure 5-2B), so that your right IT band (fascia or band of tissue reaching from your hip to your shin) is stretched from where it connects to the knee up to where it connects in the hip.
E) Reverse steps A-D for your other leg (Figure 5-2C).
F) Walk forward repeating steps A-E for 30 meters.

Figure 5-2A

Figure 5-2B

Figure 5-2C

ARM SWINGS WITH ELASTIC BANDS

Motivation: There is nothing better than performing a drill with the same motion as race walking. The single best arm exercise for race walking is to practice the motion of the race walker's arm swings with elastic bands so that you use your hips properly. The enhanced arm swing forces a greater forward rotation of the hips.

Steps

- A) Wrap an elastic band around a pole and place each end in your hands.
- B) Swing the hands back and forth through the full range of motion traveled while race walking.
- C) Counter your arm swing by pushing your opposite hip forward.
- D) Remember to keep those shoulders relaxed!
- E) Repeat for 2 to 10 minutes.

Figure 5-3A

Figure 5-3B

 ## LONG STRIDES - LONG ARMS DRILL

Motivation: If you are having difficulty feeling the proper motion of the hips, try this drill.

See chapter 4, page 33 for steps to complete this drill.

 ## FOOT PLANT DRILL

Motivation: When you switch which leg is supporting your weight, the *Foot Plant* drill emphasizes the forward hip rotation in a very localized motion.

See chapter 4, page 46 for steps to complete this drill.

TIM'S STRETCH

Motivation: Since Tim doesn't remember where he learned this stretch or what it was called, he now claims it by his own name. Good hip flexor range of motion is a key to good forward hip rotation.

Steps:

A) Sit on the floor with your weight resting on a bent right leg as shown in Figures 5-4A and 5-4B.
B) Place your left leg behind the body and bend it at the knee to 90 degrees.
C) Use your right elbow to support your upper body weight.
D) Raise your left elbow above the head and arch your back, while also slightly pushing your left hip forward.
E) Repeat with your right side of your body.

This gives a nice long line to follow from the left hip to the left elbow, allowing for a great stretch from the left hip flexor all the way up to the left triceps.

Figure 5-4A

Figure 5-4B

TALES FROM THE TRACK

We've all seen those athletes who start the race much faster than the pace their bodies can sustain. After a time in front of the pack, they fall far out of contention by the finish. Maybe you've been guilty of that error yourself once or twice because you were caught up in the excitement of the competition. I can tell you from experience, if you can avoid this trap and race within yourself, it will pay off big time.

Tim Seaman and I learned this firsthand at the 2004 Athens Olympics. We started the 20km race conservatively, which landed us in dead last for the first several kilometers. As hard as it was to be patient in last place at the Olympics, Tim and I stuck to our plan. As the kilometers ticked by, we caught more and more athletes. By the end of the race, we passed over half the field, including powerful walkers from Russia, China, and Mexico. Having ice in our veins led to the best Olympic race of our careers as well as the fastest finish by Americans at the Olympics ever.

—*Kevin Eastler, two-time Olympian*

SIDE STRETCH

Motivation: This drill provides a good stretch from your left knee where the IT band connects to the left elbow. Stretching this area facilitates good forward hip rotation.

Figure 5-5

Steps:

A) Stand with both feet together.
B) Grab your right elbow with your left hand.
C) Bend your left knee while keeping the right knee straight.
D) Hold for 20-30 seconds.
E) Return to the vertical position.
F) Repeat 2-3 times on one side, then switch and repeat on the other side.

ADVANCED SIDE STRETCH

Motivation: Another version of the side stretch that stretches the side and IT band greatly.

Steps:

A) Stand with your legs crossed over each other, but your feet together.
B) Grab your left elbow with your right hand.
C) Bend your right knee while keeping the left knee straight.
D) Hold for 20-30 seconds.
E) Return to the vertical position.
F) Repeat 2-3 times on one side, then switch and repeat on the other side.

Figure 5-6

IT BAND STRETCH

Motivation: Here's another stretch for the IT band. It's important to find a stretch that works for you as a tight IT band not only restricts forward hip rotation, but can lead to knee injuries as well.

Steps:

A) Stand with one leg crossed in front of the other (Figure 5-7A).
B) Bend down as you would to stretch the hamstring (Figure 5-7B).
C) Place your hands together and come halfway up (Figure 5-7C).
D) Lean toward the side of the body in which the leg is in front to feel the stretch in the opposite IT band (Figure 5-7D).

Figure 5-7A

Figure 5-7B

Figure 5-7C

Figure 5-7D

CORRECTING EXCESSIVE HIP DROP

Excessive hip drop is a funny issue for some race walkers. Part of the problem could be a misconception as to how the hip moves. While it has to move up and down, many race walkers falsely assume that it should be a more excessive movement. For those walkers, correcting the problem is simply a matter of relearning the proper motion. Other walkers, however, suffer from a lack of strength in the hips which causes the excessive drop. Often, when the hip drops, it also sways outward. While these two motions could occur independently, they are usually observed together. The hip sway compensates for the drop in center of gravity that is caused by the hip drop. Observe the following images showing proper and improper hip drop and hip sway.

Olimpiada Ivanova of Russia demonstrating proper hip drop on her way to a silver medal at the 2006 20km World Cup.

Eszter Bajnai of Hungary demonstrating excessive hip drop.

Katie Stones (#59) of Great Britain demonstrating less hip drop than Déspina Zapounídou (#67) of Greece whose hip drop is excessive. Note that these walkers are at a different point in their stride than Ivanova and Bajnai.

STRAIGHT LINE WALKING DRILL

Motivation: A side effect of rotating your hips forward is that your feet land in a straight line. Therefore, when you practice race walking along a straight line, your tendency to sway outward with your hip is reduced.

Steps:

A) Race walk along a straight line, such as a lane divider of a track.
B) Focus on your hips, reaching forward as the advancing leg swings forward.

Figure 5-8A

Figure 5-8B

CLAM SHELL EXERCISE

Motivation: The *Clam Shell Exercise* strengthens your hip abductors to prevent your hip from dropping excessively.

Steps:

- A) Lie on your side.
- B) Position your legs so that they are in a clam shell position (Figure 5-9A).
- C) Raise and lower the upper leg, maintaining the V (Figure 5-9B).
- D) Repeat 2-3 sets of 10 with the same leg.
- E) Repeat with the other leg.

For an added effort, place a light weight on the upper leg as shown in Figure 5-9C.

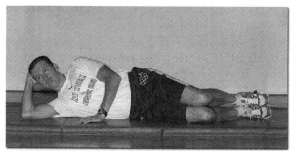
Figure 5-9A

Figure 5-9B

Figure 5-9C

BRIDGE WITH BALL EXERCISE

Motivation: This exercise strengthens the lower back muscles and upper hamstrings. This is a complementary exercise that helps but is not specific to one hip rotation problem.

Steps:

A) Lie on your back.
B) Place your feet on an exercise ball.
C) Place your hands at your side (Figure 5-10A).
D) While exhaling, raise your butt from the floor and hold for 2 to 3 seconds (Figure 5-10B).
E) While inhaling, lower your butt back to the floor.
F) Repeat 15 times; do 2 sets.

Figure 5-10A *Figure 5-10B*

TALES FROM THE TRACK

In 2004, when I qualified for the Olympic Games in Athens, I was pretty excited. As I packed and planned my training, it was difficult to shake the pre-trip jitters. Even after I arrived in Greece and settled into our training camp in Crete, I found myself very nervous about the race. While things went well in camp and the course layout was comfortable, I couldn't shake the anxiety. When race day came, I warmed up on the practice track and was corralled to the holding room with the other competitors. I went from feeling warm and ready to go, to being cold and tight as we were forced to wait for 40 minutes. Instead of letting panic set in, I looked around and realized everyone else was in the same situation. No one had an unfair advantage over anyone else. When we finally got out to the track and lined up to start the race, I looked up into the stadium and found myself looking around and trying to take it all in. As I looked at all my competitors, I realized something profound; they were all the same people I had raced against my entire career. Somehow, I thought that when I got to the Olympics it would be different, that people I had never seen before might crush me in the race. However, it was a race just like any other. The 20km distance was the same. There were fewer of us, but otherwise the athletes were the same. When I finally realized this race wasn't different after all, my nerves went away. The gun went off and I ended up walking a decent race while having a great time.

—*John Nunn, 2004 Olympian, Athens, Greece*

ELASTIC BAND LEG STRAP EXERCISE

Motivation: The *Elastic Band Leg Strap Exercise* strengthens your hip abductors to help in preventing your hip from dropping excessively.

Steps:

A) Place an elastic band around your lower legs and stand in a partial squat position with your legs a shoulder's width apart.
B) Slowly walk from side to side (Figure 5-11B).
C) Move a few side steps in one direction, then a few steps back in the original direction.
D) Take caution to make sure that each foot moves the same distance on each step.

Repeat 10 times.

Figure 5-11A

Figure 5-11B

LONG STRIDES - LONG ARMS DRILL

Motivation: If you are swaying to the side instead of driving your hip forward, resynchronize your hips by doing the *Long Strides – Long Arms* drill.

See chapter 4, page 33 for steps to complete this drill.

SIDE STRAIGHT LEG RAISE EXERCISE

Motivation: For those with excessive hip drop, this simple exercise strengthens the hip abductors without the need to go to the gym. Weak hip abductors are one reason the hip may drop excessively in race walking. This exercise can be done with or without a light ankle weight. Start without weight and gradually add light weights, building up to but never exceeding 10 percent of your body weight.

Steps:

A) Start by lying on your side with both legs extended out straight (Figure 5-12A).
B) Slowly raise the top leg, while keeping it straight, to about 45 degrees (Figure 5-12B); hold it there for a second, and then gradually lower it.
C) Repeat this exercise 15 times with one leg, then switch and repeat with the other leg.

Figure 5-12A

Figure 5-12B

LOWER SIDE STRAIGHT LEG RAISE EXERCISE

Motivation: For those with excessive hip drop, this simple exercise strengthens the hip adductors without the need to go to the gym. Weak hip adductors are one reason the hip may drop excessively in race walking. This exercise can be done with or without a light ankle weight. Start without weight and gradually add light weights, building up to but never exceeding 5 percent of your body weight.

Steps:

A) Start by lying on your side with the lower leg extended out straight and the upper leg bent in a triangular position as shown in Figure 5-13A.
B) Slowly raise the lower leg, while keeping it straight, to about 15 degrees (Figure 5-13B); hold it there for a second, and then gradually lower it.
C) Repeat this exercise 15 times with one leg, then switch and repeat with the other leg.

Figure 5-13A

Figure 5-13B

HIP FLEXOR STRETCH - LUNGE FORWARD

Motivation: Tight hip flexors inhibit proper forward hip rotation.

Figure 5-14

Steps:

A) Place your right knee on the ground with your right foot extended behind you.
B) Place your left foot on the ground in front of you, making sure the left knee stays behind the ankle (Figure 5-14).
C) With a straight back, lunge forward and feel the stretch in your right hip flexor.
D) Hold for 20-30 seconds.
E) Repeat 2-3 times on each side.

PIRIFORMIS STRETCH

Motivation: The piriformis is a muscle located within the glutes. Due to the excess hip rotation of a race walker's stride, this muscle tends to tighten, which can lead to an injury known as piriformis syndrome.

Steps:

A) Lie on your back.
B) Place your left foot on your right knee.
C) Lift your right knee up so that your thigh is perpendicular with the ground.
D) Grab your leg under the knee and pull the leg toward you.
E) Hold for 20-30 seconds.
F) Repeat 2-3 times with each leg.

Figure 5-15A

Figure 5-15B

HIP FLEXOR STRETCH - ADVANCED

Motivation: Tight hip flexors inhibit proper forward hip rotation.

Figure 5-16A

Steps:

A) Kneel on the ground, preferably softer ground than tough man Tim has selected in the photos.
B) Place your left leg in front of the body while bending at the knee.
C) Lower your torso, using your hands for support (Figure 5-16A).
D) Slide the right leg back and lower your torso all the way down so that your forearms are supporting your body weight (Figure 5-16B).
E) Feel the stretch across your right hip flexor and left piriformis.
F) Hold for 20-30 seconds.
G) Repeat 2-3 times for each side.

Figure 5-16B

Chapter Six
Leg Issues

While chapter 4 details leg issues as they correspond to a violation of the definition of race walking, chapter 6 focuses on leg issues pertaining to efficiency. While these issues do not directly lead to disqualification, they rob you of effectiveness and therefore need to be corrected.

 CORRECTING HIGH KNEE DRIVE

Walking with a high knee drive is fraught with problems. While you may be walking with one foot in contact with the ground at all times, a high knee drive may make you appear to lose contact. Even if you are not getting disqualified, you still need to be concerned about wasted energy by moving your leg up and down further than necessary. The leg is approximately 15 to 20 percent of the body's weight, so lifting it higher than necessary approximately 20,000 times during a 20km race wastes a lot of energy.

Additionally, a high knee drive, as illustrated in Figures 6-1A and 6-1B on the next page, gives you the appearance of running instead of having a fluid movement. Your head may also bounce up and down, creating an added jarring motion in your stride and potentially increasing your chance of injury.

Figure 6-1A *Figure 6-1B*

FOCUS ON: Quicker Lower Leg Swing

Instead of driving your leg forward with the top of your leg leading the way, once the knee passes under the torso focus on swinging the lower leg and foot as fast as possible until your heel strikes the ground.

FOCUS ON: Swinging Your Feet Like a Broom

One method to get your knees lower is to think of your swinging foot like a broom, sweeping as low to the ground as possible. Studies have shown that the higher the foot is swinging through the stride, the more likely the athlete is to get loss of contact violations.

FOCUS ON: Lowering Your Knee Drive

While it may sound obvious, to prevent a high knee drive, focus on keeping your knee low. When the leg swings forward and the knee drives upwards, it gives the appearance of loss of contact.

SCUFF WALKING DRILL

Motivation: By dragging your foot along the ground, you are training your body not to drive the knee high. Once the body is accustomed to walking with low foot carriage, you can raise the foot slightly and will be race walking with perfect foot carriage.

Steps:

A) Walk slowly, swinging the foot so low that you scuff your toes on the ground as they move forward.
B) Do this for 30 to 50 meters. Do not scuff your feet for an entire lap or through a full workout.

Figure 6-2A   *Figure 6-2B*   *Figure 6-2C*

Figure 6-2D   *Figure 6-2E*   *Figure 6-2F*

FOOT PLANT DRILL

Motivation: One side effect of high knee drive is that you carry your foot through too high as well. By practicing the *Foot Plant* drill, you repeat the action of your foot swinging low to the ground. Really focus on foot placement when doing this drill to correct high knee drive.

See chapter 4, page 46 for steps to complete this drill.

HIP FLEXOR STRETCH - LUNGE FORWARD

Motivation: Tight hip flexors make it difficult to maintain a long stride behind the torso, due to the associated lack of hip rotation. Therefore, the rear foot lifts off the ground prematurely, often causing a high knee drive. To prevent this, make sure that your hip flexors allow a greater range of motion.

See chapter 5, page 81 for steps to complete this drill.

HIP FLEXOR STRETCH - ADVANCED

Motivation: In addition to the *Hip Flexor* stretch, this advanced stretch may be used to further improve forward hip rotation and thus reduce high knee drive.

See chapter 5, page 81 for steps to complete this drill.

CORRECTING OVERSTRIDING

Overstriding in front of your body makes it difficult to walk efficiently and can lead to the perception that you've lost contact with the ground. A tight hip flexor causes the rear foot to lift off the ground prematurely and shortens the stride where you want it the longest. In addition, overstriding may be caused due to poor arm swing or just overly zealous effort (usually when you are tired and muscling through).

FOCUS ON: Shortening Arm Swing

Work on shortening your arm swing so that the hands come back to at most 4 to 6 inches behind the hips. The arms, hips, and legs all move in rhythm and are proportional. A decrease in arm swing should reduce your stride length.

Some people incorrectly profess that the peak of the upper arm's range of motion should be when the upper arm is parallel to the ground. Instead, the peak of the upper arm's range of motion should come when the upper arm is making a 45-degree angle with the body.

FOCUS ON: Forward Hip Rotation

Often overstriding in front of the body is caused by a lack of forward hip rotation. Concentrate on driving your hip forward to reduce the percentage of your stride that is in front of your torso.

 **FOOT PLANT DRILL**

Motivation: Part of the problem with overstriding is that your foot dangles out in front of the body, neither pushing nor pulling your body forward. If you more effectively place your foot just in front of your body, your stride becomes more efficient.

See chapter 4, page 46 for steps to complete this drill.

 QUICK STEPS - HANDS BEHIND BACK DRILL

Motivation: Any of the *Quick Steps* drills can be added to your routine to correct overstriding. If you choose one, the *Quick Steps – Hands Behind Back Drill* is best. If you have time, do the other varieties as well as they will also improve your turnover rate.

See chapter 4, page 62 for steps to complete this drill.

 LONG STRIDES - LONG ARMS DRILL

Motivation: Any stretch or drill that improves the range of motion of the hip flexors will reduce overstriding.

See chapter 4, page 33 for steps to complete this drill.

 HIP FLEXOR STRETCH - LUNGE FORWARD

Motivation: Any stretch or drill that improves the range of motion of the hip flexors will reduce overstriding.

See chapter 5, page 81 for steps to complete this drill.

 HIP FLEXOR STRETCH - ADVANCED

Motivation: Any stretch or drill that improves the range of motion of the hip flexors will reduce overstriding.

See chapter 5, page 81 for steps to complete this drill.

 CORRECTING A WIDE STANCE

When pedestrians walk quickly, they rarely change their technique; they merely walk with a more exaggerated stride at a faster cadence. This gets them only so far or fast. Race walkers, in contrast, change many aspects of their stride, most notably adding a forward drive of the hip as the leg swings forward. Most race walkers who walk with a wide stance do so because they do not rotate their hips forward and therefore inward. Since the hip cannot move forward in a straight line, it must rotate inward as it rotates forward. As it does, it causes the foot to land along a straight line.

Figure 6-3, Wide Foot Stance

To correct a wide stance, you can perform any of the corrections for incorrect hip rotation as taught in chapter Five. In addition:

> **FOCUS ON:** Bringing Your Arms to the Center
>
> Focus on bringing your arms to the center point in front of your body in line with your sternum. Synchronize the placement of your feet, so that they land "underneath" your hands.

> **FOCUS ON:** Forward Hip Rotation
>
> It may seems that we keep repeating hips, hips, and more hips, but they are key to many problems with race walking technique. If your feet are not landing in a straight line, it is probably due to a lack of forward hip rotation. When the hip rotates forward, it also rotates inward, causing the feet to land in a straight line. Concentrate on driving your hip forward and you will naturally straighten out your foot placement.

STRAIGHT LINE WALKING DRILL

Motivation: When trying to correct a wide stance, one can encourage the hips to rotate forward by walking along a straight line. It is important to note that your footfalls land in a straight line as a result of proper hip rotation and not just forcing your feet to land along a straight line without any rotation of the hips.

See chapter 5, page 76 for steps to complete this drill.

FOOT PLANT DRILL

Motivation: The *Foot Plant Drill* focuses your attention on the proper way to place your foot down.

See chapter 4, page 46 for steps to complete this drill.

CORRECTING FOOT AND KNEE CROSSOVER

While it's fairly rare to see a race walker cross one foot over the other, it does happen. In fact, we used to speak of it hypothetically until at a recent clinic, a young beginning race walker who lacked the muscle control to keep his legs and feet in line demonstrated this problem as part of his stride. While there are no specific exercises to correct this, use the following two points to correct crossover problems.

Figure 6-4, Foot and Knee Crossover

> **FOCUS ON: Shortening Arm Swing**
>
> Focus on walking on a straight line. If you are crossing over the line, then you are wasting effort to the side instead of driving yourself forward.

> **FOCUS ON: Forward Hip Rotation**
>
> Swiveling your hips around the axis that runs through the middle of your body is **not** desirable. Hip motion must be primarily forward. Extend your hip forward as the leg swings forward. Minimize the inward rotation.

STRAIGHT LINE WALKING DRILL

Motivation: Since foot and knee crossover is largely due to lack of muscle control, walking along a straight line refocuses your technique.

See chapter 5, page 76 for steps to complete this drill.

SIDE STRAIGHT LEG RAISE EXERCISE

Motivation: Strengthening the abductors in conjunction with the *Lower Side Straight Leg Raise Exercise* will increase your control as you place your foot on the ground.

See chapter 5, page 80 for steps to complete this drill.

LOWER SIDE STRAIGHT LEG RAISE EXERCISE

Motivation: Strengthening the adductors which in conjunction with the *Side Straight Leg Raise Exercise* will increase your control as you place your foot on the ground.

See chapter 5, page 80 for steps to complete this drill.

FOOT PLANT DRILL

Motivation: The *Foot Plant Drill* focuses your attention on the proper way to place your foot down.

See chapter 4, page 46 for steps to complete this drill.

CORRECTING IMPROPER SWING FOOT CARRIAGE

A very common problem for race walkers is the circumduction on the swing foot as it travels forward after push off. This is seen in Figures 6-5A through 6-5C.

Figure 6-5A *Figure 6-5B* *Figure 6-5C*

The cause of a race walker's circumduction varies greatly. It can be many muscle inbalances or a tightness in many areas. It is most likely to be a weakness or tightness in the hip abductor, hip flexor, quadriceps, hamstrings, or anterior of your shins. A coach can best assess the exact cause and can recommend the specific exercise to correct it.

TALES FROM THE TRACK

Life doesn't always play fair. I was in the best shape of my life when I walked the A standard in preparation for the 2004 Olympic Trials. A poorly timed illness led me to a second place finish at the Olympic Trials. Due a convoluted series of regulations, I did not qualify for the Olympic Team. Beside the great personal disappointment, it was my children's frustration with the system that was harder to handle. My kids were still at an age where they thought good people who work hard achieve their goals. When I decided to continue and a similar fate became of my World Championship birth, my kids really questioned the fairness of the situation. "Mom, This is so terrible how can this be happening to you again?" I explained that if this is the worst problems we have, then I am living a pretty blessed life. By continuing through to the 2008 Olympic Trials and having things finally fall into place, my qualifying for the Beijing Games taught my kids and myself a valuable lesson. While there are no guarantees in life, sometimes when you work hard, your dreams do come true.

—*Joanne Dow, Fastest time ever by an American woman at the Olympic Games*

Chapter Seven
Arm, Hand, and Shoulder Issues

When creating a PowerPoint presentation for our clinics we sifted through countless photographs and selected examples of good and bad arm technique by elite walkers. While there were plenty of examples of both, when we sorted them and placed the best and worst side by side, a pattern appeared. Almost all the examples of the best technique were photographs of non-U.S. race walkers, and most of the examples of the worst technique were from U.S. walkers. This sobering realization should be a wakeup call to American walkers. You must focus on your arms if you want good technique. Indeed, I could even see the progression (in the wrong direction) of some athletes' style over the years.

Observe a few of the comparisons we found:

Irina Petrova demonstrating textbook arm carriage at the 2006 20km World Cup.

Samantha Cohen demonstrating high arm carriage at the 2004 20km Olympic Trials.

Eric Tysse showing the hand down and behind the hip.

Michelle Rohl showing arms too high and tight.

Tim Seaman's right hand is below and behind, exactly where it should be.

John Nunn's right hand is too high.

Keeping your arm close to the body as Korzeniowski (#2679) does is critical to efficient arm action.

CORRECTING ARM CARRIAGE ISSUES

There are many ways to vary from the ideal arm carriage. Race walkers can carry their arms:

- Too high
- Too low
- With no rotation
- With excessive cross over the torso
- With a lack of range of motion

Fortunately, the cures are basically the same for all these ailments.

FOCUS ON: Below and Behind

Bringing your hand back below and behind the hip is essential to achieve proper arm motion, as well as to make it easier to reach forward with your hips. If your arms do not reach back far enough, they will not come forward to the proper position. In addition, your hip drive is diminished. To increase the range of motion through which your arms and hands travel, increase the angle between your upper and lower arm. To decrease the range of motion through which your arms and hands travel, decrease the angle between your upper and lower arm.

FOCUS ON: Brushing Your Shorts

When swinging your hands forward and back, you should not swing them far from the side of your torso. If you hold your hands too far out, you waste energy supporting the weight of your arm. To get your hands closer to the proper position, brush your shorts lightly with your hand.

FOCUS ON: The Chest Line

Many walkers violate this concept on both sides of the imaginary line across your chest. While there is some variation in the ending height of the forward arm swing, a good goal for the point of the arc is your chest line. If your hands are swinging above the line, then increase the angle that your forearm makes with your upper arm. In contrast, if your hands aren't swinging high enough, then decrease the angle your forearm makes with your upper arm.

FOCUS ON: A Constant Angle

The arm swing should maintain a constant angle between the forearm and upper arm. Do not pump your arm as it swings forward and back. Resist the temptation to close the angle on the upswing and open the angle on the downswing.

> **FOCUS ON:** *Hand Shaking*
>
> When you reach forward to shake someone's hand, your hand moves forward on an arc from the side of your hip to cross the front of your body. It should do the same in race walking. The only difference is that when you shake someone's hand, your arm angle does change, whereas in race walking the arm angle remains constant.

BICEPS STRETCH

Motivation: While race walkers do not pump their biceps muscles during race walking, they do use them to hold the arm in approximately a 90-degree angle. Go for a long enough walk and your biceps will get tight.

Figure 7-1

Steps:

A) Stand up with your feet shoulder width apart.
B) Place your hands together, behind your back, with your palms together as in Figure 7-1.
C) Exhale while raising your arms until you feel the stretch.
D) Hold for 15 seconds.
E) Lower your hands.
F) Repeat three times.

TRICEPS STRETCH

Motivation: Inflexible triceps muscles cause a reduction of arm angle, leading in turn to a reduction in hip rotation.

Figure 7-2

Steps:

A) Stand up straight with your feet shoulder width apart.
B) Bend your left arm back so that you touch your hand to your shoulder.
C) Grab your left elbow with your right hand.
D) Gently pull your left arm backwards as in Figure 7-2.
E) Hold for 15 seconds.
F) Repeat with your other arm.

ARM SWINGS WITH ELASTIC BAND EXERCISE

Motivation: This exercise is the same as the one taught in chapter 5. It strengthens the arms in a manner specific to race walking. While you can do weights to strengthen your biceps, triceps, etc., this drill is far more effective due to its functional nature.

See chapter 5, page 71 for steps to complete this drill.

CORRECTING HAND ISSUES

Heather Buletti demonstrating a lack of focus that led to a floppy hand during the 2006 World Cup.

Hand carriage during race walking is quite simple. Simply keep a straight wrist with the hand in a loose fist. As your hands pass by your hips, the fingertips face the hips. However, many race walkers' hands flop all over the place, drawing a judge's watchful eye as well as wasting energy. There are really no exercises to help; it's primarily an issue of focus.

FOCUS ON: Closed Hands
Think about closing your hands, but do not make a fist, while you are walking.

FOCUS ON: The Stick
Either imagine or actually place a small stick inside your fist. Focus on keeping your hand and fingers from swaying up, down, or side to side. Coach Peña used this little trick on Andrew Hermann and it helped him walk his way onto the 2000 Sydney Olympic team.

FOCUS ON: The Chip
Too tight a fist wastes energy and leads to a tense body. Imagine that you are carrying a potato chip between your thumb and your index finger. By imagining the chip there and that you must not break it, you'll relax your hand position without letting the hand flop about.

CORRECTING SHOULDER ISSUES

The most common problem with race walkers' shoulders is tightness resulting in high shoulder carriage. This also leads to a high arm carriage and increased chance of getting a lifting call, due to your increased center of gravity.

In addition, tight shoulders could lead to cramps, making it difficult for you to maintain proper arm swing. Once your arms stop swinging, your hips are sure to follow. Once you lose your hips, you will be pedestrian walking the rest of the way. Curt Clausen credits finally learning to relax his shoulders as the key to improving his arm swing and thus freeing up his hips. This technique improvement was a key factor in Clausen's bronze medal at the 1999 World Championships in Seville, Spain.

FOCUS ON: A Low Center of Gravity

When your arm swings forward and back, focus on your elbows. Keeping your elbows down lowers your center of gravity and improves your arm swing.

TALES FROM THE TRACK

To have fulfilled my childhood dream of becoming a world champion was an experience I will never forget, and one which is not lost on me either. Few athletes have reached the pinnacle in their chosen sport, and to add my name alongside the athletes before me, I count myself extremely fortunate.

The road to success in the 50km world champions in Osaka was fraught with more downs than ups during the 2007 season, contrary to what my results may show. After I carried a slight niggling injury into the race in December 2006, where I set a new world record for the 50km walk (3:35:47), a more serious injury would strike in the weeks following, which saw me miss the entire Australian domestic season and races early in the European season.

My first race for the season was the IAAF Challenge meet in La Coruna in June, where a solid time of 1:19:37 left me reasonably satisfied but more optimistic about what may be around the corner. However, akin to my previous toeing of the start line, I developed an injury in the week following which threw some doubt over my preparation for the World Championships. Although I missed approximately 4 weeks post-World Cup, an important training block, I recovered in time to head to a training camp in St Moritz, Switzerland, and train solidly but not outstandingly. I was, however, confident in my preparation, in addition to both my work earlier in the year and the fantastic base I have from years of high level training. Positive reinforcement is crucial and is definitely a constant factor for me, whilst accepting that injuries occur and are just an added challenge to the life of an athlete.

I arrived in Osaka for the World Championships from Europe 10 days before my race, a short acclimatization period but, as I have always performed well in both the heat and humidity, a period I felt to be sufficient. I remember vividly the morning of the 50K race and the feeling of confidence I had whilst warming up. Prima facie, I believed I was the athlete to beat, having proven myself previously on the international stage and being the current World Record holder. It was just a matter of execution. On my arrival at the call room, my coach Craig Hilliard reinforced these sentiments to me: "You're the best! Go out there and prove it!"

(Continued on page 101)

BACKWARDS WINDMILL DRILL

Motivation: When the body is cold, this drill is a great way to get blood pumping to all extremities quickly. In addition, it helps to relax and stretch the upper body (specifically targeting the shoulders), leading to a more fluid arm motion.

Steps:

A) Start with one arm at your side and the other pointed straight up to the sky (Figure 7-3A).
B) Swing the arm at your side up and forward at the same time as you swing the pointed arm back and down (Figure 7-3B).
C) Allow both arms to make circles, keeping your arm close to the side of your head as you swing it back (Figure 7-3C).
D) Walk with the proper lower leg motion of race walking.
E) Perform this exercise for 30 meters. (Figures 7-3D through 7-3F complete the cycle.)

Figure 7-3A

Figure 7-3B

Figure 7-3C

Figure 7-3D

Figure 7-3E

Figure 7-3F

REVERSE WINDMILL STRETCH

Motivation: The *Reverse Windmill Stretch* is a great way to warm up the shoulders and increase your range of motion at the same time.

Steps:

A) Begin by placing one hand on your shoulder, arm relaxed, elbow toward the ground (Figure 7-4A).
B) Slowly raise the elbow forward so that the arm becomes perpendicular to your body (Figure 7-4B).
C) Continue bringing the arm straight up, keeping your biceps as near to your face as possible.
D) Slowly rotate the arm back with the elbow as close to your body as possible (see Figure 7-4C), aware that it must travel outward at some point.

Figure 7-4A   *Figure 7-4B*   *Figure 7-4C*

E) As the elbow passes behind your head, keep your upper arm parallel to your shoulders (Figure 7-4D).
F) Gradually rotate the arm through a complete circle (Figures 7-4E and 7-4F) and return to the original position. Slowly repeat the rotation ten times with each arm.

Figure 7-4D   *Figure 7-4E*   *Figure 7-4F*

STATIC SHOULDER STRETCH

Motivation: A good stretch to add to your cool down is the static shoulder stretch. It helps to relax the shoulders after a walk.

Steps:

A) Attempt to clasp your hands behind your back, one from above and one from below, as shown in Figure 7-5A.
B) If you can reach, hold the position for 20 to 30 seconds.
C) Reverse arms to stretch the other shoulder.
D) If your hands remain a few inches apart from each other, use a towel to complete the stretch (see Figure 7-5B).
E) Walk your hands up the towel, positioning them as close together as possible, then reverse arms.

Figure 7-5A

Figure 7-5B

TALES FROM THE TRACK

(Continued from page 98)

Post factum, I believe I controlled the race well, staying close to the front of the lead pack and covering the moves of athletes I'd highlighted to myself beforehand to watch. At 35km, still some distance to the finish, I made what turned out to be the winning move, and not long afterwards I knew victory would be mine.

It's a strange feeling knowing for such a long period of time that you're going to win the World Championships; the sheer length of the 50K makes it one of the few events where once your final move has been made, you can relish victory for the final kilometers. What a luxury! Ironically, the feeling of relief outweighed happiness initially. However, there's no better feeling in the world than to carry your country's flag on a victory lap. That's one feeling I want to experience again!

—*Nathan Deakes, 2007 World Champion, 2004 Olympic Bronze Medalist*

NECK STRETCH

Motivation: Tight neck muscles lead to high shoulders and a higher center of gravity. If only one side is tight, your head could tilt to one side.

Steps:

    A) From a seated or standing position, place your palm against the side of your head (Figure 7-6A).
    B) Gently push your head to the side so that your ear moves closer to your shoulder (Figure 7-6B).
    C) Hold for 10-15 seconds.
    D) Repeat with the other hand in the opposite direction.

Figure 7-6A

Figure 7-6B

Chapter Eight
Posture Issues

Stand up straight! How many times have you heard that? It sounds easy, but it isn't always easy to accomplish. In ideal race walking posture, the torso is in the vertical position. Some race walkers never achieve this position, while others develop problems when they become tired late in races. Posture problems fall into two main categories: leaning forward and leaning backward.

CORRECTING LEANING FORWARD

Forward lean is very undesirable in race walking. It can be caused for many reasons, including poor coaching. The main physical causes are tight abdominal muscles, overdeveloped or tight pectoral muscles, weak lats (the biggest back muscle group), and/or a weak lower back.

FOCUS ON: Head Position

Your posture often follows your head position. If you drop your head, your posture is sure to follow and you will slouch forward. When you race walk, focus on keeping your head up. Pay attention to your chin as well. Keeping it up helps to bring your posture upright as well as allowing your airway to stay open, letting your body get maximum oxygen when the going gets tough.

FOCUS ON: Looking Forward

If you look down at the ground, it's sure to affect your posture. Instead, look down the road. Don't look at the ground directly in front of you. Your peripheral vision will pick up any dangers on the road.

FOCUS ON: A Vertical Line

Many race walkers are not aware of the problems with their posture. By using a treadmill and mirror you can determine if your posture is up to snuff. Make a vertical line on the mirror to show where your body should be when you are walking on the treadmill. Focus on walking (positioning the mirror to the side of the treadmill) while keeping your body even with the line.

BACK EXTENSION MACHINE EXERCISE

Motivation: For those with a healthy back, a back extension machine strengthens the lower back to hold you in a good upright posture and helps to correct leaning forward.

Steps:

Since there are many different types of back extension machines, follow the instructions at your local gym. Please do not do this exercise if you have back problems. See Figures 8-2A and 8-2B for the intended motion.

Figure 8-2A

Figure 8-2B

ALTERNATE ARM AND LEG EXERCISE

Motivation: This simple exercise doesn't require a gym or even weights. It strengthens the lower back muscles as well as the glutes, upper hamstrings, and to some degree the shoulders and thus helps to correct forward lean.

Steps:

- A) Lying on your stomach, hold your arms and legs straight out.
- B) While exhaling, raise one arm and the opposite leg five inches from the floor (Figure 8-3A). Be sure to keep them straight.
- C) Inhale as you lower your limbs.
- D) Exhale while raising the opposite arm and leg, keeping them straight (Figure 8-3B).
- E) Inhale while lowering your limbs.
- F) Repeat, 2 sets of 10.

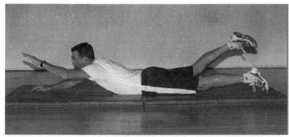

Figure 8-3A

Figure 8-3B

 ## SUPERMAN EXERCISE

Motivation: This exercise is a bit more advanced than the *Alternate Arm and Leg Exercise*, but it also strengthens the lower back muscles as well as the glutes, upper hamstrings, and to some degree the shoulders.

Steps:

- A) Lying on your stomach, hold your arms and legs straight out as shown in Figure 8-4A.
- B) Simultaneously, exhale and raise your arms and legs five inches off the floor (Figure 8-4B). Be sure to keep them straight.
- C) Hold for 3 seconds.
- D) Inhale as you lower your arms and legs.
- E) Repeat 15 times.

Figure 8-4A

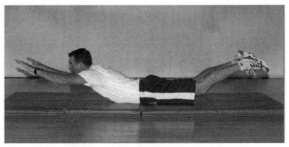

Figure 8-4B

LAT PULLDOWN MACHINE EXERCISE

Motivation: This exercise helps to correct leaning forward because if your lats aren't strong enough, your torso will be pulled forward by your abdominal muscles. This is especially true for people who have done a lot of abdominal work while neglecting their back.

Steps:

A) Sit in front of a lat machine.
B) Grab the bar with your palms facing away from you, and place your hands at end of the bar (Figure 8-5A).
C) Pull the bar down in front of your body.
D) Lower the bar all the way down to past your chest (Figure 8-5B).
E) Return the bar back to the top, stopping just before your arms completely straighten.
F) Keep control while raising and lowering the weight. Don't let the bar swing back excessively as you return to a starting position.
G) Perform 10 repetitions for 3 sets.

Figure 8-5A

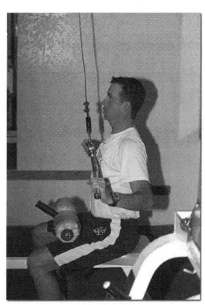

Figure 8-5B

ROWING MACHINE EXERCISE

Motivation: If you already have strong pectoral muscles (located in your chest), a rowing machine balances by strengthening your rhomboids (located in your upper outer back, between your shoulder blades and your spine). Strengthening your rhomboids pulls you upright so that you don't lean forward.

Steps:

A) Sit on the seat of a rowing machine and grab the handles of the machine with straightened arms (Figure 8-6A).
B) Pull back on the cable(s), keeping your back straight (Figure 8-6B).
C) Lower the weight, straightening your arms.
D) Repeat steps B and C 10-15 times for 3 sets.

Figure 8-6A

Figure 8-6B

BRIDGE WITH BALL EXERCISE

Motivation: Another great exercise to correct forward leaning without having to go to a gym is this exercise which works the back extensors.

See chapter 5, page 78.

PEC STRETCH

Figure 8-7

Motivation: Tight pectoral muscles pull your shoulders into a forward, rounded posture, thus causing you to lean forward as you race walk. This exercise loosens them.

Steps:

A) Stand in a doorway.
B) Place one arm against the doorway, holding your arm at an 80-degree angle with the side of your body. Bend your arm at your elbow at 90 degrees if necessary (Figure 8-7).
C) Lean forward, maintaining a vertical body alignment, until you feel the stretch across your pecs.
D) Hold for 30 seconds.
E) Repeat five times on each side.

COBRA STRETCH

Motivation: This stretch corrects leaning forward if your abdominals are tight. It stretches them into extension.

Steps:

A) Lie face down, extending your legs behind you with your feet together (Figure 8-8A).
B) Place your hands on the side of your body, even with your shoulders.
C) Keeping your legs on the floor and feet flat, push your body up while exhaling (Figure 8-8B).
D) Hold for five seconds.
E) Lower your body down while inhaling.
F) Repeat ten times.

Figure 8-8A

Figure 8-8B

STANDING BACK STRETCH

Motivation: This stretch corrects the problem of leaning forward due to tight abdominal and back muscles. It does so by stretching them into extension.

Steps:

A) Stand with your feet shoulder width apart.
B) Place your hands behind your back (Figure 8-9A).
C) Lean backwards (Figure 8-9B).
D) Hold for two seconds.
E) Return to the upright posture.
F) Repeat ten times.

Figure 8-9A

Figure 8-9B

CORRECTING LEANING BACKWARD

People lean backward for many reasons. The major culprits are weak abdominal muscles and a tight lower back. Both of these conditions lead to inefficient race walking style, but more importantly they can lead to injuries and lower back pain. While it may take a while to correct this problem, it is time well spent, because the benefits from the following exercises will not only help your race walking, but also help you walk better in your daily life.

 ## BALL RAISE EXERCISE

Motivation: This exercise strengthens the abdominals and shoulders, helping to prevent leaning backwards.

Steps:

A) Hold an exercise ball in front of your body (Figure 8-10A).
B) Exhale while you raise the ball to the height of your forehead, making sure to keep your back straight.
C) Continue to exhale as you hold the ball in place for 2-3 seconds.
D) Inhale while you slowly lower the ball to your waist.
E) Tighten your abdominals as you raise the ball.
F) Repeat 15 times.

Figure 8-10A

Figure 8-10B

TRADITIONAL STOMACH CRUNCHES

Motivation: The *Traditional Stomach Crunches* are a very basic method of strengthening your abdominal muscles without overly stressing your back. Strong abdominal muscles help to prevent a backward lean.

Steps:

A) Start by lying down on a firm surface.
B) Bend your knees and bring both feet toward your buttocks, so that your legs form a triangle with the ground (Figure 8-11A).
C) Place your hands across your chest, and begin to curl upward by tucking your chin to your chest.
D) Slowly roll your upper body off the ground (as much as eight inches), pressing your lower back to the ground as you curl (Figure 8-11B).
E) Always exhale while curling your body upward.
F) Hold for three seconds.
G) Lower your body to its original position by reversing your movements and inhaling as your body lowers to the ground.
H) Repeat the exercise as many times as possible (up to a maximum of 100 crunches), but only as long as you can maintain good technique.

Figure 8-11A

Figure 8-11B

BICYCLE EXERCISE

Motivation: The *Bicycle Exercise* puts a literal twist on the *Traditional Stomach Crunch* in that it adds a twisting motion to work a greater range of abdominal muscles.

Steps:

- A) Start by lying down on a firm surface.
- B) Touch your right elbow to your left knee, lifting your torso up slightly as you do (Figure 8-12A).
- C) Simultaneously lower your raised elbow and knee while raising the opposite knee and elbow (Figure 8-12B).
- D) Repeat the exercise 25 times.

Figure 8-12A

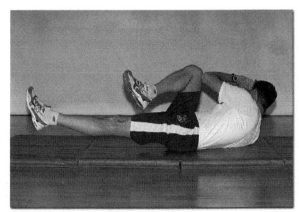

Figure 8-12B

UPPER BACK STRETCH

Motivation: This exercise allows you to get more comfortable posture and remove your backward lean by stretching your upper back.

Figure 8-13

Steps:

A) Wrap your hands around a pole, standing far enough back that your arms are straight.
B) Lean backward, feeling the stretch through your upper back (Figure 8-13).
C) Hold for ten seconds.
D) Repeat three times.

KNEES TO CHEST STRETCH

Motivation: This is a simple, comfortable way to stretch the lower back and remediate a backward lean in your posture.

Figure 8-14

Steps:

A) Lie down on your back.
B) Place your hands on the lower hamstrings, just before their insertion point to the knee.
C) Pull your knees towards your chest and hold for 30 seconds (Figure 8-14).
D) Repeat five times.

PRAYER STRETCH

Motivation: A simple, comfortable way to stretch the lower back and help remediate a backward lean in your posture.

Figure 8-15

Steps:

A) Kneel on the floor, with your knees hip width apart.
B) Use your hands for support, placing them shoulder width apart.
C) Lower your head.
D) Slide back to a seated position with your buttocks on your heels.
E) Stretch forward, reaching out with your hands as in Figure 8-15.
F) Hold for 30 seconds.
G) You can alternate by walking your hands to each side.
H) Repeat five times.

TALES FROM THE TRACK

When I donned the Team USA colors for the second time in international competition at the Barcelona Olympic Games, I had no idea what I was in for. It was like a dream. My years of training and previous competitions had brought me to this threshold and now I was here for the big dance. In Barcelona, meeting the other athletes, in particular other race walkers, was the key to setting up my athletic career for the next four years. One such encounter occurred at the practice facility within the Olympic Village. I was about to start my 1,000m repeats when Canadian race walking legend Guillaume LeBlanc's coach asked me what I was doing. When I told him, he asked if I could time my repeats with Guillaume's 5,000m repeats. It worked out perfectly. As I did my repeats, Guillaume would sit right behind me stride for stride. I finished my 6 repeats (4:00, 4:00, 3:59, 3:59, 3:58, and 3:56) and he simultaneously hit two 5km's with sub-20 times. I marveled at his incredible workout exactly one week before the 20km final. Guillaume went on to capture the silver medal, while I finished 32nd out of 42 starters. I even beat former Olympic champion Ernesto Canto, who had stayed at my house 14 years before. The best part of the whole experience was that, after the race, Guillaume thanked me for pulling him through that workout! He felt that it gave him the confidence and edge he needed to win that medal. Despite my loss in this race, his gratitude turned the experience into a winning moment in my memory.

— *Allen James, two-time Olympian*

Epilogue

We end *Race Walk Clinic – in a Book* with a simple graph that illustrates how to balance speed with technique. If you walk too fast, your technique suffers and your risk of disqualification is high. On the contrary, if you focus too much on textbook technique, you speed naturally slows and your performance suffers. It's all about balance. Balance your training, technique work, and remedial drills and your performances will soar.

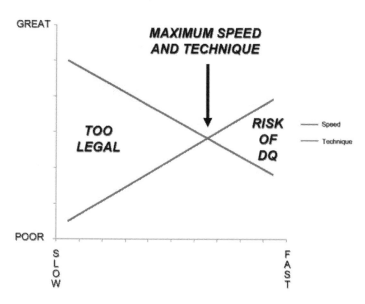

Additional Publications by Walking Promotions

If you are reading this page, you clearly are already interested in race walking and have a strong knowledge of the sport. How about inspiring one of the 75 million baby boomers who need to learn about our great sport? *BoomerWalk* is written to inspire a wide range of people to become race walkers. It is a great summary of basic technique that motivates readers to get off the couch and start race walking. Author Brent Bohlen relates his experience in discovering the sport of race walking at a time in his life when his aging knees no longer could take the pounding of his four-decade love of basketball. Race walking provided him the cardiovascular fitness he needed, the competition he wanted, and the kindness his knees demanded. Once he convinces you to take up race walking, whether for fitness or for competition, Bohlen provides the basics of race walking technique to get you off on the right foot. You can begin race walking right away with no special equipment.

Order from www.BoomerWalk.com, www.racewalk.com, or www.amazon.com for $15.95 + S&H.

Printed with 8 1/2 x 11 full-color pages, *Race Walk Like a Champion* is the single best compilation of information on the technique, training, and history of race walking. It combines approximately 400 photographs with charts and diagrams to explain every detail of race walking.

Race Walk Like a Champion starts with a thorough explanation of how to select race walking shoes and warmup; it then describes every aspect of race walking technique, judging, and training philosophy in extensive detail. Other chapters include stretching, racing, strength training, mental preparation, injury treatment, and nutrition. *Race Walk Like a Champion* also includes a comprehensive chapter on the history of American race walking. Each era of walking is described with an introduction and biographies of that period's greats.

Order from www.racewalk.com for $23.95 + S&H

The *Race Walk Like a Champion* companion DVD/CD brings the descriptions from the book to life while explaining all aspects of race walking in DVD-quality video. However, the benefits of the DVD format do not end there; the interactivity makes it a coach in a box. Its friendly menus allow you to watch exactly the section you wish, over and over, with no rewinding! Have a technique problem? Just drill down through the interactive menus and your everpresent coach is there to assist.

Order from www.racewalk.com for $49.95 + S&H

Made in the USA
Lexington, KY
14 June 2019